W9-BDF-389

DEEP IS THE HUNGER

DEEP IS
THE HUNGER

Meditations for

Apostles of Sensitiveness

by

HOWARD THURMAN

RICHMOND
INDIANA

Library of Congress Cataloging in Publication Data

Thurman, Howard, 1899 —
  Deep is the hunger.

  Reprint of the 1951 ed. published by Harper, New York, which was an expan-
sion of the author's Meditations for apostles of sensitiveness, published in 1948.
  1. Devotional literature. I. Title. II. Title: Meditations for apostles of sensitiveness.
[BV4832.T558 1973]   242   73-16023
ISBN 0-913408-10-7

Copyright, 1951, by Harper & Row, Publishers, Incorporated

Published by Friends United Press
101 Quaker Hill Drive, Richmond, IN 47374

To

The Resident Members and Members-at-Large

of

The Church for the Fellowship of All Peoples

CONTENTS

vii

PREFACE

My custom is to write a weekly meditation for the calendar of the Sunday services at our church. As a result of many requests, fifty of these meditations were first published in 1947, followed, a year later, by a second edition which included fifty additional meditations. The response has been such that a third edition, greatly enlarged, is now being sent forth to reach an even wider audience. Included in this edition is a special group of twenty-five "working papers," which we have used in the thirty-minute meditation period which precedes the service each Sunday morning. It is hoped that they will find a place of meaning in the lives of those who, though not a part of our service, share profoundly in the same quest and hunger for God.

The title, *Apostles of Sensitiveness,* was used as the subject of an address which I gave at the Cathedral of St. John the Divine in New York City in February, 1946, under the auspices of the Interracial Fellowship of Greater New York. I am deeply of the mind that there is a need for materials of refreshment, challenge and renewal for those who are intent upon establishing islands of fellowship in a sea of racial, religious and national tensions. My experiences in sharing in the development of a church dedicated to so crucial an undertaking underscore very simply the character of the desperate need for resource materials; that is the demand which called into being these paragraphs. The attempt is not to set forth a connected series of observations or reflections, but rather to throw a shaft of light on aspects of thought, of life, of religious experience, as they are encountered in the daily round.

Appreciation is due and gladly acknowledged to those who typed and retyped the manuscript: Mrs. Elizabeth Buchanan, Miss Leila Bohall, Miss Marjorie Branch, Miss Louise Bessett and Miss Leila Hinton; and to Miss Julia Lee and Miss Grace Marrett who read the entire manuscript and gave many helpful suggestions. A very special word of appreciation to Miss Adena Joy, assistant minister of the Church, without whose technical skill, incisive mind and editorial wisdom the manuscript in its present form would not have been possible.

HOWARD THURMAN

November, 1950
The Church for the Fellowship of All Peoples
San Francisco

Concerning Apostles of Sensitiveness:

"And it is my prayer that your love may be more and more rich in knowledge and all manner of insight, enabling you to have a sense of what is vital . . . ."; thus writes the Apostle Paul to the Church at Philippi. To have a sense of what is vital, a basic and underlying awareness of life and its potentialities at every level of experience, this is to be an Apostle of Sensitiveness.

I

A Sense of History

THERE is a universal urgency for both personal and social stability. This urgency can find fulfillment along several lines. A fresh sense of history must be developed. All the events of our world must be placed in a context of incident that reveals their profound interrelatedness. History on this planet must be regarded not as individual happenings unrelated to social processes, but, instead, as overlapping patterns of group behavior brought into play by a wide variety of creative personal and impersonal forces at work in the world. History is not irrational; it has a deep logic and consistency. God is the God of history. He does not stand apart as some mighty spectator but is in the process and the facts, ever shaping them (in ways that we can understand and in ways beyond our powers to grasp) to ends that fulfill a great and good destiny for men. This is no idle or pious wish. Examine the past and behold the unfolding of living process.

1.

EVERYBODY knows that something has happened. Just when it happened, no one knows. But there is complete agreement that somewhere, something very important has given way and all sorts of things are pulled out of shape, or are sagging or falling apart. The results? Nerves! There is a sense of fear as of some impending doom around the next turning in the road. There seems to be a climate of disaster that does not quite materialize into cataclysmic incident; only a general loss of morale. Explanations abound. Some say that we are caught in the open independence of the sea, far away from any port, and a storm of world revolution is upon us. They point to the breaking up of century-old social patterns all over the world. India is free for the first time in centuries and deep within that freedom there is the division of Pakistan and Hindu. Nevertheless, the ferment within the country could not be stopped by half-measures; the great mass of Untouchables, by a stroke of the pen, are given freedom of movement and person within the wider political and social freedom of the country itself. Illustrations may be multiplied from the ends of the earth as well as from within our own country. Who would have dreamed that a report like "To Secure These Rights" would have been projected and produced by the Democratic party, the party of the Solid South? There is the fact that we have passed through a period of total war. Always in the past, war has been the specialized function of a particular group within the state, set up and organized for the purpose. But total war is new. By total war is meant that every man, woman and child in the state was somehow involved—also that every conceivable resource of the national life was involved—that every social force was oriented to that end. This meant, and continues to mean, that no one may claim detachment. The result is deep strains and stresses in the soul of a people, for which they had no preparation and from which there seems to be no sure basis for recovery. One could go on to call attention to the development and use of the atomic bomb. Many persons are sure not only that the development of the bomb marked the initiation of a new era for mankind but that it also killed something precious in the life of the race.

2.

THERE is much discussion concerning what seems to be an increasing restlessness among people. This restlessness takes many forms. Sometimes it appears in easy irritation over matters of little or no consequence. Sometimes it results in the sudden rupturing of old ties of family, job and friends. It may be a general instability making for an unwillingness to assume responsibilities and to fulfill obligations. In its simplest and often most crucial form, it makes concentration on anything difficult because of an apparent futility. One of the reasons for this restlessness is not far to seek. During the past decade, the world has gone through a series of tremendous social upheavals, upsetting the equilibrium of the daily lives of millions of people everywhere. What has happened in Russia,

Europe, Asia, the Orient and the United States has been more than the mind could adjust to without leaving in its wake a residue of impending uncertainty and, perhaps, even doom. In addition, there is upsetting of the balance in nature, whose children we are, by the far-reaching effects of atomic research and developments. This development has undoubtedly communicated to the physical organism a subtle unbalance creating overtones of ill-at-easeness in the mind and in the consequent behavior of us all. The list is by no means exhausted. But there is a deeper restlessness that belongs to the very structure of personality. "Always roaming with a hungry heart," this is man in his essential nature. This characteristic has been and continues to be a primary concern of religion. Sometimes it is referred to as the "divine discontent" in the heart. Certain mystics call it the "homing instinct" in the human spirit. One characterizes it as the "flight of the alone to the Alone." The classic expression of it in Christianity is the oft-quoted overtone from Augustine, "Thou hast made us for thyself and our souls are restless till they find their rest in Thee." A modern poet suggests that God gave to man every gift but *rest* so that man would never be at ease, finally, except with God. In quietness and meditation, one must distinguish between the two dimensions of restlessness so as not to confuse them. After all, they may be one and the same. To the man who has found his rest in God, there comes the strength to reduce all the ill-at-easeness to manageable units of control, making for tranquility in the midst of change and upheaval.

6

3.

W HAT are the conditions under which men tend to lose their nerve? It is obvious that men tend to lose their nerve in the presence of experiences that inspire fear and imminent danger. Under such circumstances, the loss of nerve may be a sheer automatic reaction of the nervous system, the heritage of a million years of the struggle of life to survive on the planet. Men lose their nerve sometimes when they are forced to make sudden and crucial decisions involving their destiny and the destiny of others. This means that the responsibility of decision is more than a single individual is willing to undertake on his own. Of course, the opposite effect sometimes occurs. Men whose entire past has been characterized by shiftlessness and weakness find themselves faced with a decisive moment requiring nerve and firmness, and, under the stress of the moment, become courageous and daring. It is not particularly difficult to handle a loss of nerve where the facts surrounding the circumstances are clear cut and definite. A man knows what he is dealing with and draws on all of the resources of his personality to rise to the occasion. Where the loss of nerve is a result of a general breakdown in society it is infinitely harder to manage. The classic illustration is to be found in the closing days of the Roman Empire when the average Roman citizen had lost his sense of responsibility for the fate of the Empire. Everywhere there was a sense of impending crisis. A period, somewhat similar in effect, is upon us. We are rapidly becoming a nation of panic-ridden people. The present tendency is to make of everyone a scapegoat for our collective fears. This means that we are losing our sense of destiny as a people and are relaxing our faith in the ideals which gave birth to our nation and for whose high fulfillment we have in the past marshaled the resources of our common life. We cannot fight an idea with threats, investigations and scares. We can fight an idea only with a greater idea, to which, in all phases of our life, we are dedicated with high purpose and deep resolve. This is the answer to our present loss of nerve.

4.

HAVE you ever been in a position in which you had to stand up and be counted? Really! For most of us life does not make the specifically dramatic demand of taking a formal stand. A friend of mine, a teacher in a certain divinity school, found himself in a faculty split over a special issue involving one of his colleagues and students. Eventually the board of trustees became involved in the affair. Then, one day, all members of the faculty had to take a position, for or against. To be *for*, meant to be on the side of the trustees. The issue could not be dodged; a position had to be taken. My friend took a positive stand on an issue that was vital to him and his security, for the first time in his life. His convictions put him on the side of the minority. The next fall, he was teaching at another school. In commenting on the situation he said, "For the first time in my life, I felt that I was a man. It was the first time that I could not hedge, but instead I had to take sides in accordance with the integrity of my convictions without regard to possible consequences. I became a new person, way down deep." Of course, there are people who are always taking positions, always declaring themselves, always being counted. For such, perhaps, the dramatic character of "stand taking" is neutralized by repetition. They are professionals. There is a very important contribution made to all causes by such people. The burden of our thinking has to do with what happens when a person is pulled out of the regular routine of his life by some issue and finds himself standing up to be counted. It is a crucial experience. It means that a person is willing to take full responsibility for his actions, actions that extend beyond his little world, actions which may involve him in risk, foreign both to his temperament and to his life plan. We are living in the midst of events that make such demands upon us. The options often are very few. It is well within the possibility of the present that we shall be called upon to take a stand which will be, for us and our kind, decisive, in terms of the life and death of the person. It may not be a bad idea to get in practice now and to develop the climate within, that makes it possible for you to make up your mind—to be counted!

5.

SOMETIMES it takes a lifetime to determine whether or not a single act was a mistake or not. There are some acts that carry with them a swift and decisive judgment. Their effect is immediate and traceable. I lose my temper and as a result use words in speaking to another that can never be recalled. The effect is unmistakable and I cannot take them back.

> Boys flying kites haul in their white winged birds;
> You cannot do that when you are flying words.
> Thoughts unexpressed may fall back dead
> But God Himself can't stop them once they're said.[1]

Much of life involves us in actions growing out of decisions that work out their fulfillment through many months and often years. It is a simple but terrible truth that, in most fundamental decisions which we make, we must act on the basis of evidence that is not quite conclusive. We must decide and act on our decision without having a complete knowledge even of the facts that are involved. What we do is postpone decisions as long as we can, getting before us as many relevant facts as possible. Then there comes the moment of decision and we act. Our hope is that the future will reveal the rightness of our decision but we are never quite sure. Think back over your own life. Are there things that have befallen you that are the result of wrong decisions? At the time, you did not think they were wrong. Or perhaps you could not wait longer for further investigation and exploration. Your evidence was not sufficient but it was all that you could secure, the situation being what it was. Now you see what you could not have seen fifteen years ago. It has taken all these years for you to discover that you were mistaken. Since life is this way, it is most unwise to make decisions, destiny-dealing decisions, with half a mind or in a casual manner. Since, at our best, we must act again and again

[1] "The First Settler's Story," from *Over the Hill to the Poor-House and Other Poems* by Will Carleton (New York: Harper & Brothers).

on the basis of inadequate evidence, it is quite unworthy of our responsibility as human beings to use less than our highest wisdom in making up our minds. There is no guarantee that the decision I make will not, in the end, form a mistake, a bad judgment, a movement in error. But I shall bring to bear upon it the fruits of my cumulative wisdom in living, the light from as many lamps along the way as I can see, and the greatest spiritual resources available to me. It has taken more than a thousand years to determine whether the death of the Son of Man on a cross outside the city wall was a mistake. It was madness; but with that madness Jesus discovered a new world.

6.

"No one ever wins a fight"—thoughtfully, and with eyes searching the depths of me, my grandmother repeated the words. I was something to behold. One eye was swollen, my jacket was ripped with all the buttons torn from their places, and there was a large tear in the right knee of my trousers. It was a hard and bitter fight. I had stood all I could, until at last I threw discretion to the winds and the fight was on. The fact that he was larger and older and had brothers did not matter. For four blocks we had fought and there was none to separate us. At last I began to gain in power; with one tremendous effort I got him to the ground and, as the saying went, "made him eat dirt." Then I had come home to face my grandmother. "No one ever wins a fight," were her only words as she looked at me. "But I beat him," I said. "Yes, but look at you. You beat him, but you will learn someday that nobody

ever wins a fight." Many years have come and gone since that
afternoon in early summer. I have seen many fights, big and
little. I have lived through two world wars. The wisdom of
these telling words becomes clearer as the days unfold. There
is something seductive about the quickening sense of power
that comes when the fight is on. There is a bewitching something men call honor, in behalf of which they often do and
become the dishonorable thing. It is all very strange. How
often honor is sacrificed in defense of honor. Honor is often
a strange mixture of many things—pride, fear, hate, shame,
courage, truth, cowardice—many things. The mind takes many
curious twistings and turnings as it runs the interference for
one's survival. And yet the term survival alone is not quite
what is meant. Men want to survive, yes, but on their own
terms. And this is most often what is meant by honor. "No
one ever wins a fight." This suggests that there is always some
other way; or does it mean that man can always choose the
weapons he shall use? Not to fight at all is to choose a weapon
by which one fights. Perhaps the authentic moral stature of a
man is determined by his choice of weapons which he uses in
his fight against the adversary. Of all weapons, love is the most
deadly and devastating, and few there be who dare trust their
fate in its hands.

7.

It is a source of constant wonder how trees seem to take the
measure of the climate and make of their existence a working paper on life. Along some parts of the coast where there

is a steady wind from the sea, there is a general recognition of the fact that it is extremely difficult for trees to grow tall and straight against the sky. Yet they do. They bend with the wind and ride out every storm, yielding only enough to guarantee themselves against destruction. It is a very fine art, this bending with the wind and keeping on. Of course, the winds leave their mark. The trees are not upright as if they have never known the relentless pressure of many winds through many days. One sees, sometimes, trees that have grown in a community of trees where there is mass protection of many trunks for those not on the outer rim. Such trees have flattened tops. The trunk may be tall and straight, gaining every available inch of shelter all the way up, until at last there is the point where the topmost branch feels the pull of the sun and the sky to go its way alone. Here there is no single branch. Doubtless many have tried, but in the process have been snapped off, leaving their bleeding stumps as a mute testimony to heroic worth. The tree soon learns its lesson: within the resources available to it, a little canopy of branches inch their way above the protecting wall of other trees. They are young and supple, they bend with the wind, always sustained by the sturdy growth from which they have come. Unless the wind is able to sever them from the main body of the tree, their continued growth is guaranteed. The tree seems to say to the branches, "Bend with the wind but do not release your hold, and you can ride out any storm." To the trees that did not learn how to bend with the wind but preferred rather to remain straight and defiant against the sky and are now dead and rotting in the earth, it was a great moment when they came crashing to the ground with a certain sense of triumph: "Ah, it took the concentrated violence of all the winds of heaven to bring me low. Such is the measure of my strength and my power." There is a strange, naked glory in the majesty of so grand a homecoming. All through the life of man on the planet, there have been sun-crowned men like that, and around them movements for the healing of the nations have arisen. And yet man, in the mass, has continued to survive because he has learned to bend with the wind.

8.

"BEND with the wind and keep on living." This exhortation raises the basic question of compromise. It can be interpreted to mean that so high a premium is placed upon survival for its own sake that to do *anything* in order to survive is quite all right. Compromise, as an ethical issue, is often very difficult to settle. It is of the very essence of certain kinds of idealism to take the position that compromise, in any form and under any circumstances, is never to be countenanced. This presupposes that it is possible for an individual to live in society wihout some measure of compromise. For many, the word compromise is too strong; a softer and more "scientific" term, such as adjustment, is used. A man does not make a compromise in a given situation; he merely adjusts. When the tree bends with the wind, it is merely adjusting itself to its environment without any real loss. The fact that it grows into many grotesque shapes that are a denial of its true pattern of growth is considered unimportant. The main business of the tree is to keep alive, bear seed so that it can reproduce itself and thus fulfill its destiny. This idea suggests that fundamental to the notion of compromise is some understanding of the ends which are sought. Therefore, it is quite reasonable to say that a man may deal in compromises in matters that to him are not really important; while in matters that to him are at the center of meaning, he is unyielding. Life may be like a battle. The chief strategist selects the point at which he elects to take his stand, and retreats and charges until at last he jockeys the enemy into the position where the definite line of real battle can be drawn. The analogy is inadequate, but the principle is clear—a man must decide *where* he draws the line beyond which he will not yield. Taking a position involves a profound spiritual dilemma, because it exposes the individual to the necessity to be somewhat apologetic because he draws the line at one point while some of his fellows draw it at another. On the other hand, in taking his position he acts as if he is infallible, with all the overtones of arrogance and pride, though his very spirit rejects any notion of pride in himself for doing what to him is simply the right thing. A careful examination of any man's life would reveal that, at one point he bends with the wind and keeps on living, while at another point he defies the wind and is quite prepared to be brought crashing to the ground.

9.

In the town of Lany, twenty-five miles outside the city of Prague, there are four unmarked graves. They are the resting places of the three Masaryks and Eduard Benes. A friend who was there stated that, some months before his death, Dr. Benes visited the cemetery. He expressed a desire to be buried alongside his friends and compatriots. It was also his desire that the grave should go unmarked. "For," said he, "if the people love me, I shall live in their hearts and they will never forget the place of my grave; hence an identification is unnecessary. If they do not love me, I shall be forgotten in their hearts; and the most elaborate tombstone will make no difference." The same principle is illustrated by a letter which one man of letters wrote to his friend about a new book which the friend had written. The book contained many lengthy quotations from a wide variety of other writers. "Why do you quote so many authorities in your new book?" wrote the friend. "If what you have said is true, you do not need the authorities; if what you are saying is not true, all the authorities in the world will not make it true." These accounts raise the whole question of the value of living life seriously, as contrasted with taking life seriously. The man who believes simply in life and is willing to work at his job, whatever it may be, with simple integrity of purpose and honesty of effort, does not waste his energy worrying about whether he will be remembered or forgotten, whether others will sanction his truth or not. Of course, it is perfectly natural for a person to want to be remembered, to be kindly thought of, or to have his ideas sanctioned by others who are supposed to know. But in the last analysis, the basis of truth is within and not without. A man who depends upon externals for his significance, who must look to others for the nod of the head, is one whose life is constantly at the mercy of whatever it is he is courting in his environment. He can very easily become the victim of envy and jealousy. Often, he ends up by stretching himself out of shape in trying to be to others what he can never be but what someone else could be without trying. Where do you place your emphasis?

10.

"ALL living structures are organized with reference to functions." This is an observation that is scientific as well as commonplace. It calls attention to the fact that every living thing is so made that it is geared to do the things that will make its continuing to live quite possible and normal. The ear is a delicate instrument fashioned by infinite patience so that the hearing of sound is possible; and so with the various organs of man, the living organism. What is true of man is true of the other forms of life. I have watched often how my plants shift the angle of their leaves so as to get a maximum exposure to the sun. The point is obvious and need not be labored. All of this means that life is purposive in the sense that it is functional. When the emphasis is shifted from the physical organism to the mental and the spiritual, many people find it difficult to see the application of the same basic principle. Very often, the mental life seems so chaotic, so filled with random movement, so utterly irrational, that it is extremely difficult to see that the mind itself is *organized* with reference to function. When the same principle is applied to human behavior, the picture becomes even more disconcerting. And it is only when we pass ethical judgment upon human behavior that the picture becomes acutely puzzling. It is true that human behavior is purposive. But to identify purposiveness with morality may seem to stretch the point. But if it be true that what applies to the human organism applies equally well to the total life of man, then we are under tremendous obligation to seek to know and understand the meaning of the functioning of human life at every level and in all of its manifestations. The quest for such understanding is the meaning of the human enterprise. When a man discovers this for his personal life, he has found what religion calls the Will of God for his life. Men find this by the intense application of all of their cumulative knowledge and wisdom to the solution of the personal problem and, in so doing, discover something of the larger meaning of life. No man is spared from this necessity; it establishes a kinship among men that transcends language, creed, vocation, sex, color, and all of the temporary devices by which one man is separated from another.

11.

THE Angel with the Flaming Sword is a striking figure of speech as well as a very accurate bit of symbolism. George Fox used it to symbolize the guardian angel placed at his post by divine order. We are all of us brought into direct contact with the Angel. He works in many strange and well-nigh mysterious ways. There are times when we adopt a particular course of action in accordance with a series of powerful, urgent and right desires. Step by step, we make our way; one thing leads to the next, and on and on until at last we are brought face to face with the fateful moment, the climactic act. Then, time stands still, the whole pattern of one's life is brought to bear upon the crucial act; something happens; we do not go through with it; the Angel with the Flaming Sword has made his presence known. It is more than conscience, more than mere conflict between right and wrong, more than simple violation of what one was taught to hold true. The Angel is the symbol of the Eternal sitting in judgment upon the temporary and the passing; the combination of rushing wind, flashing lightning and still small voice. No man can go past the Angel and remain as he was before the searching encounter. Dreadful indeed would it be if the Angel were withdrawn from your life. He is the guardian of all your ultimate values, the keeper of the seal of your spirit, the guarantor of all your meanings. When your decisions are finally made, the Angel says "Yes" or "No" and, upon his nod or frown, turns your destiny. Of course, he can seem to be ignored, but every man knows deep within him that he cannot escape his tryst with the Angel. It is well to be full of thanksgiving that the Angel with the Flaming Sword guards the ultimate treasure and secret of the life of man. He is sustainer of the essence of your life and mine and our final protection against the dissolution of the integrity of life. It is small wonder that George Fox felt that, when he came up past the Angel with the Flaming Sword, all the world had a new smell. There is no more graphic meaning put into the word *hell* than this—the Angel with the Flaming Sword is on the war path in the human spirit—the Angel with the Flaming Sword is on the war path in the soul of a people—eternal guardian, great contender, mighty bulwark, God's wall of fire in and for the life of man.

12.

I have often wondered about the brother of the prodigal son, the brother who stayed at home. The point of the story as Jesus told it throws the spotlight on the son who broke his father's heart by going away and who returned after many days. There was profound reconciliation between him and his father. The moral is: however far one may stray from God, reconciliation with God is always possible, and when it takes place there is great rejoicing. What about the boy who did not go away? He was a bit unimaginative. He had a deep sense of loyalty and had made his peace with his lot. So at-one was he with the smooth operation of the family that he was taken for granted. The father knew that he would have nothing to fear from that son. His word was dependable. He was industrious, and devoted. When the hot-blooded, volatile brother returned, having exhausted his resources and energies far afield, a feast was prepared, fine linens placed on his person and the father's signet ring on his finger. Returning from the field, the boy who had stayed at home heard the rejoicing and the celebration. When he came into the presence of his father, he saw his brother. What a moment! All sorts of impulses· shook his frame. Doubtless he said to himself, "What a fool I have been! There is no reward for devotion, for being true to my standards. Look at him! I feel the smirk in his soul; he is saying, 'Why don't you get wise to yourself, older brother? I ate my cake and I have it too. There was a time when you wanted to see the bright lights, and experience the gaiety of the city, but always you repressed yourself, and now you've grown old, tired, and bitter.' " Aloud, he said to his father, "I have been with you all the time, but you have never even given me a birthday party. If I had the energy left, I could hate you; I've given you the best days of my life, and no thanks." The father was shocked, and, under the pressure of his elder son's withering judgment, he expressed his love for him. It had never occurred to him before to say to his son how precious he was to him. On the other hand, these words may characterize the older brother: "There are [people] in the world to whom the joy and the sorrow come alike with quietness. For them, there is neither the cry of sudden delight nor the cry of sudden anguish. Gazing deep into their eyes, we are reminded of the light of dim churches. . . . They are the [people] who have missed happiness and know it, but having failed of affection, give themselves to duty."

13.

PERHAPS the simplest definition of art is that it is the activity by which men realize their ideals. The assumption is that it is the nature of ideals to seek to realize themselves, to seek to become a part of the facts of experience. It may be argued that an ideal that does not seek to realize itself fades out, grows dim and finally disappears. We must not permit too hasty a judgment here. To be sure, there are some ideals that are much slower in their realization than others. Until the rise of Hitler in Germany, it was a commonplace remark that political and social ideals take many years before they can realize themselves in the lives of the people. (One of the secondary watchwords of Democracy was that it takes a long time for the ideals of democracy to realize themselves in the lives of the people.) Hitler demonstrated, for all to see, that within considerably less than a single decade, practically an entire nation could become committed to the realization of an ideal of the state which was contrary to previous patterns of behavior in very important and strategic respects. This suggests that, when the ideal is brought into focus in the mind of the individual or the people of a state and held there with sufficient intensity over a time interval of sufficient duration, the ideal tends to realize itself in the very life of the people. We are all artists in the sense that we are all engaged in some kind of activity by which we are realizing our ideals. What kind of ideals are you realizing? There is no neutrality here. Everybody is engaged in this activity. Is what you are realizing worthy of you, or are you engaged in the realization of ideals of which you are ashamed, and before which you stand condemned in your own sight? Long, long ago, it was said by a very wise and understanding friend, "By their fruits ye shall know them"; *not by their roots.*

14.

THE fact that a man can always be in error with reference to the things that he thinks he understands most clearly is an ever present reminder of human frailty. It is a challenge to humility even in the presence of one's deepest convictions. The truth is we are never able to get our hands on all the facts in a given situation; something that is important always escapes our consideration and may lead us to a false conclusion honestly arrived at. The fact that it is honestly arrived at may not alter the fact that the conclusion is false. We are all creatures of limitation and it behooves us to recognize this fact at every point. This does not mean that we are excused for our errors due to a lack of knowledge, experience or patience. But it does mean that even when we have done our best thinking, our most honest probing of our own motives, plumbed the depths of our innermost cumulative experience of living, we may arrive at a point less than the right. If this is true, then carelessness in attitudes, slovenly thinking, half-hearted attempts at understanding, all these are simply without justification. Each person is under obligation to do, to the limit of his powers, the very best thinking, the most honest feeling of which he is capable, as he faces even the simplest alternatives of life. The constant reminder of our limitations is but one of the ways in which God affirms in human life that we are His children and He is our Father. In His presence and His presence alone there is the calm assurance that even the limitations of our "frame" provide Him with abundant levels of expressions of His love toward us and His fulfillment in us.

15.

AT an Institute on Education in Human Relations sponsored by the National Conference of Christians and Jews in Cleveland, Ohio, Dr. Howard Wilson of Harvard University made a most significant address on the bearing of intergroup relations on international issues. He made four pointed suggestions well worth reflecting upon in the profoundest manner possible:

1. We need more facts, more information, more objective experience in intercultural relations.
2. We must find some means for sympathetic communication with other people.
3. We must find some means for better understanding of other people.
4. There is a desperate need for conversation, the exploration of whole new areas of experience through the medium of shared conversing.

Many people think that they understand others when they merely maintain a kindly attitude toward them. While it is true that a generous mood toward other people again and again elicits a response of friendliness, this is no substitute for facts, for information and the kind of understanding which comes only from sustained natural exposure to others. This constant exposure is apt to be a sure check and corrective to one's understanding. Intergroup relations are handicapped by awkward and clumsy means of communication. Often this is a matter of language, of our use of words, of our use of anecdote and accent. There is no more exacting enterprise than the conscious quest for precise communication between people. How can I make my meaning clear to you, how can I reveal myself to you so that my understanding of you will be a self-revelation of me? I am apt to be insensitive precisely at the moment requiring the most subtle kind of delicate feeling on my part. Often this is a lack of imagination. We can be so earnest and sincere in our grim determination to be brotherly that we are completely unmindful of the effect of our action on those whom it is our greatest desire to understand. There is such a thing as bad taste in trying to be helpful. Often our very heaviness and seriousness close doors in our faces and cause us to alienate those with whom we seek an authentic fellowship. Human understanding requires great artistry; the touch of the artist may be light, but it is sure. This is one of the reasons why conversation and good talk are of such immense value. They provide moments of direct quickening in contact that instructs the emotions and feeds the understanding with revelations of interests, slants and overtones of the other person, without which there can be no deep sure respect for personality.

16.

In one of Petrarch's Letters of Old Age appear these words:

When a word must be spoken to further a good cause, and those whom it behooves to speak remain silent, anybody ought to raise his voice, and break a silence which may be fraught with evil.... Many a time a few simple words have helped further the welfare of the nation, no matter who uttered them; the voice itself displaying its latent powers, sufficed to move the hearts of men.

It is so easy to underrate the potential power of one word spoken at the critical moment. We say to ourselves sometimes that, because we are not famous or learned or rich or powerful or gifted, our word means nothing in the presence of a great injustice. Who would pay attention to us? Many good causes are hindered, often nameless persons are brought to an untimely end, because "those whom it behooves to speak remain silent"; and because they do not speak, we do not speak. It is important to remember that there is no limit to the power of any single voice when it is the only outlet, the only channel for justice or righteousness in a given situation. The silence of the high and mighty sometimes gives greater power to the simple voice of a solitary individual. During practically any week, you may be faced with some great wrong or some simple but gross expression of injustice and there is no one to speak but you. Do not be silent; there is no limit to the power that may be released through you.

17.

THE capacity to see clearly the far reaching consequences of a particular course of action requires a quality of discipline not easy to acquire. It is to be pointed out that there are some individuals who seem to have this ability naturally as a gift of life. But these are the rare people. Most of us acquire the power of self-projection in action the long, hard way. In the first place, it requires a rather forthright honesty on the part of the individual. He must be able to sift through motives and impulses that are deep within him, or have come to focus in his mind, and understand what they are, really, in themselves, and what they will do to him and to others if they are made the basis of a course of action. These results are never visualized in their entirety but must be called to mind as fully and as honestly as possible. Here one draws on one's past experience, one's observations of others and one's cumulative experience of living. Once the results are faced, then the individual is in a position to decide whether the course of action is what he really wants at the time and whether it produces the kind of result he is willing to stand by in the future. But even this may not be enough. For sometimes—yea, often—a particular course of action may involve other people, against their will or with their consent and collaboration. Then there is the question whether the other person or persons involved will be able to manage themselves without irreparable damages. It is never enough merely to act responsibly oneself, or to be willing to pay the price for one's own deeds, but we are ever under the tireless obligation, where others are concerned, to place no burden upon others the consequences of which are not seen by them as clearly as we may see them ourselves. Despite the deep solitariness of life, in the intricate pattern of human relations no man lives to himself, nor indeed does he die to himself, or to himself alone.

18.

ONE day I saw city workmen doing an emergency job on the sewer pipes that were deep beneath the surface of the street in front of our home. As I watched the process, I was struck by the fact that about five feet of sewer pipe was completely enmeshed by a thick network of large and small roots. It was impossible even to see the section of the pipe. After much chopping and "uprooting," the pipe was uncovered—but not quite, for some of the roots had found their way inside the joints and had grown so profoundly within the pipe that it was impossible for water to flow. The whole section of the sewerage was blocked. It developed that the roots had come from a tree more than

500 feet away. Deep under the ground they had caught the scent of water from the sweating pipes and found what they sought. The book of Job says of a tree stump, "Yet through the scent of water it shall sprout again and bring forth boughs like a plant." It is always dangerous to read into the behavior of nature some great design or plan and to apply that design or plan to human life. Nevertheless it is good to know that life in any form seems to have a little way of its own, moving with quiet assurance to some special end. It is of immeasurable comfort to remember that much of the chaos and disorder of our own lives is rooted in causes that are understandable; much of the evil in life is reasonable, in the sense that its roots can be traced and it is not necessary to place the blame upon the devil or some blind senseless process. The naked responsibility for human misery, you and I and ordinary human beings like us must accept. In this doomful fact there is the ground of hope, because it means that, in the creation of man, God provided for limitless resourcefulness, and because any situation, however chaotic, can be understood and reconstructed if we have no fear to do, if need be, the radical, the revolutionary deed.

19.

THERE is a line from an old Hindu poem which says, "Thou hast to churn the milk, O, Disciple, if thou desirest the taste of butter." The line continues by saying, "And it serveth not thy purpose if, sitting in idleness, thou sayest, 'Lo, the butter is in the milk, yea, the butter is in the milk.' " The same idea is expressed in a prayer written by Sir Francis Drake in the sixteenth century: "O, Lord God, when Thou givest to Thy servants to endeavor any great matter, grant us to know that it is not the beginning but the continuing of the same until it is thoroughly finished which yieldeth the *true glory.*" There is no substitute for character in the human enterprise or in the fine high art of living. By character I do not mean mere moral excellence in the general field of conduct. But I mean the highest possible quality of excellence and authenticity in the area of the realization of ends regarded as fully desirable. An idea or an ideal can be held only to the extent that it realizes itself. No amount of pretense or formality or parading can substitute for the sheer realization in achievement of the idea, ideal or dream to which one is dedicated. This is the true test of character in the sense in which the term is used here. If a man is ill and sends for a physician, of what he wants to be most deeply assured is that the doctor has character as a physician. It is not important.at the moment whether he drinks tea or coffee, whether he parks his car on the right side of the street, whether he remembers his wife's birthday anniversary; but the crucial question is, when he sits by the bed of a sick man, "Can he practice medicine?" Only in the white heat of testing and trial, is there revealed the rugged structure of the discipline that makes for real character. It is in this sense that theory and practice can never be separated. Practice is theory realizing itself. One of the tragedies of the modern liberal is the illusion that theory and practice, the ideal and the real, can be separated from each other. The Hindu poet is right—"Thou hast to churn the milk, O, Disciple, if thou desirest the taste of butter."

20.

"BLESSED are the poor for they shall be comforted." There is another rendering, "Blessed are the poor in spirit. . . ." Very much has been written and much more has been said about the blessings of poverty. Whole movements within Christianity, as well as in other religions, have been built around the notion that poverty places an individual in a unique position to receive in large measure the peace of God. The argument runs that poverty causes a man to reduce his sponsorship of material things to the barest minimum, thereby enabling him to be free to give himself more completely to the things of the spirit. Further, poverty reduces the degree to which other men are able to threaten and to render insecure the position of the poor man. Poverty becomes then a virtue in itself. So strongly has this idea been developed that poverty is made synonymous with righteousness, purity of motives, etc. And yet, in an industrial society such as ours, poverty has been identified with disease, vice, crime, etc. The whole picture is very confusing. Years ago, I remember hearing a sermon in a large Protestant church in Evanston, Illinois, which took the position that poverty was due to laziness, to lack of thought, and therefore resulted in divine displeasure. All of these notions seem to be far removed from what Jesus had in mind in the Beatitude. He is offering the centrality of the spiritual life of man and its transcendent quality. Poverty, when voluntary, may give to the individual a power over himself that places him in a unique position to be used completely by God. To be poor in spirit is to keep oneself constantly reminded that he is not sufficient unto himself; and God is often most creatively revealed in a man's lack of strength. In moments of greatest triumph, the truly sensitive man is most profoundly aware of the vast difference between what he is and what he would be. Only "humility can never be humiliated."

21.

THE will to understand other people is a most important part of the personal equipment of those who would share in the unfolding ideal of human fellowship. It is not enough merely to be sincere, to be conscientious. This is not to underestimate the profound necessity for sincerity in human relations, but it is to point out the fact that sincerity is no substitute for intelligent understanding. The will to understand requires an authentic sense of fact with reference to as many areas of human life as possible. This means that we must use the raw materials of accurate knowledge of others to give strength and direction to the will to understand. A healthy skepticism with reference to rumors, gossip, what we read and observe about others, must be ever present, causing all these things to be evaluated by our own highly developed sense of fact. It is easy to say that we understand other persons whose culture and background are different from ours, merely because we are kind to them or willing to make personal sacrifices on their behalf. A certain Spaniard, commenting on the difference between a cat and a dog, says that a dog is direct, obvious in his expression of friendliness, while a cat, when he rubs against you is not caressing you, but merely caressing himself against you. How apropos! Unless there is a constant heightening of the sense of fact to give guidance to our will to understand, we are apt to substitute sentimentality for understanding, softness for tenderness, and weakness for strength in human relations.

22.

THE crucifixion of Jesus Christ reminds us once again of the penalty which any highly organized society exacts of those who violate its laws. The social resistors fall into two general groups —those who resist the established order by doing the things that are in opposition to accepted standards of decency and morality: the criminal, the antisocial, the outlaw; and those who resist the established order because its requirements are too low, too unworthy of the highest and best in man. Each is a menace to organized society and both must be liquidated as disturbers of the peace. Behold then the hill outside of the city of Jerusalem, the criminal and the Holy Man sharing a common judgment, because one rose as high above the conventions of his age as the other descended below. Perhaps it is ever thus. Whenever a Jesus Christ is crucified, there will also be crucified beside him the thief—two symbols of resistance to the established pattern. When Christianity makes central in its doctrine the redemptive significance of the cross, it defines itself ever in terms of the growing edge, the advance guard of the human race, who take the lead in man's long march to the City of God.

23.

THERE is no greater responsibility for the Church than to give religious instruction to its members. It is a very excellent thing to provide a place of quiet for meditation and reflection upon the meaning of life, to challenge individuals with a sense of sin and bring them face to face with their God; all of this is important and terribly urgent. But this is not enough. In a world of tremendous upheaval such as ours, where almost all of the old moorings are uprooted and it is simply maddening to try to secure and maintain one's bearing and sense of direction, the Church must be primarily a place of instruction, must include at least two important areas. In the first place, men must be taught the content of the Christian faith. Such questions as: Who was Jesus? What precisely did he teach? What are the historic Jewish-Christian insights with reference to God and the meaning of life and the interpretation of human experience? What is man and what is the nature of his responsibility? How must one interpret the true significance of the various political, economic and social arrangements under which men live? These and similar questions must be dealt with, carefully, honestly and intelligently. The second area has to do with the interior life. What is the significance of spiritual exercises? Precisely what is prayer and how does one pray? What techniques and methods are available for deepening one's sense of the presence of God and how may one work in the world courageously and intelligently on behalf of a decent world, without despair and complete fatigue? What are the resources for personal rehabilitation and renewal? That men may be able to look out on life, with all of its cruel vicissitudes and transcendent joys, with quiet eyes and tranquil spirit, is one of the end results of the attention that the Church gives to this important responsibility to the individual.

24.

YEARS and years ago—farther back than the records of history reveal—early man learned how to use a club in self-defense and thus to extend his control over an area farther than his arm unaided could reach. When he learned to throw this club with precision and power, it meant that the control of his environment was farther extended. So the story goes; as man developed—extending his arm through club, bow and arrow, gun powder, gasoline engine, through various kinds of vehicles and machines up to and including the jet-propelled plane and the atomic bomb—he had required a complete adjustment of his mind and spirit to his new power. He has been forced to fit his new powers, with each development, into a scheme of life that would keep him from destroying himself. Difficult as this adjustment has been for man's mind, it has been infinitely more difficult for his spirit and conscience. A bow-and-arrow conscience finds itself paralyzed in the presence of the cannon and the rifle. A sense of social responsibility in the use of the arrow finds itself paralyzed by the tremendous moral demands of gun powder. The dilemma of modern man is to match spiritual and moral maturity with the amazing power created by his mastery over nature. He has learned a part of the secret of energy by unlocking the door of the atom, and yet he continues to be moved by prejudice, greed and lust! He has devised a machine that can keep pace with the speed of the earth through the heavens, and yet he has not learned how to walk the earth in the midst of his fellows with simple reverence and grace. Today we stand on the verge of a brave, startling era which can yield the end of poverty, of war, and of all the breeds of hate that have made the earth a hell for countless millions. Oh, for how many years, by our deeds, shall we curse God and die, when we could reflect Him and live?

25.

A cursory glance at human history reveals that men have sought for countless generations to bring peace into the world by the instrumentality of violence. The fact is significant because it is tried repeatedly and to no basic advantage. The remark which someone has made, that perhaps the most important fact we learn from history is that we do not learn from history, is very much to the point. Violence is very deceptive as a technique because of the way in which it comes to the rescue of those who are in a hurry. Violence at first is very efficient, very effective. It stampedes, overruns, pushes aside and carries the day. It becomes the major vehicle of power, or the radical threat of power. It inspires fear and resistance. The fact that it inspires resistance is underestimated, while the fact that it inspires fear is overestimated. This is the secret of its deception. Violence is the ritual and the etiquette of those who stand in a position of overt control in the world. As long as this is true, it will be impossible to make power—economic, social or political—responsive to anything that is morally or socially motivating. Men resort to violence when they are unable or unwilling to tax their resourcefulness for methods that will inspire the confidence or the mental and moral support of other men. This is true, whether in the relationship between parents and children in the home or in great affairs of the state involving the affirmation of masses of the people. Violence rarely, if ever, gets the consent of the spirit of men upon whom it is used. It drives them underground, it makes them seek cover, if they cannot overcome it in other ways. It merely postpones the day of revenge and retaliation. To believe in some other way, that will not inspire retaliation and will curb evil and bring about social change, requires a spiritual maturity that has appeared only sporadically in the life of man on this planet. The statement *may* provide the machinery, but the functioning of it is dependent upon the climate created by the daily habits of the people.

26.

It was one of the ancient Greek philosophers who insisted that to know the right is to do it. On the basis of that idea, education, thought of in terms of increase in knowledge and in facts, is the crucial answer to social chaos. It suggests that men behave as they do because they are ignorant of the facts. Get the facts, inform thyself concerning them, and it will follow directly that a change in attitude will be in evidence. In our society, various organizations have arisen which take what is

called the educational approach to social change. There are
many people who are devoting their time and energy to the
dissemination of facts and information. All of this is to the
good and very important. The assumption is that to *know* is
to *do*. But this is a half truth, because it does not take into
account the total basis of human action. Men are not often
moved to *do* on the basis of fact alone. Have you ever heard
a person say, "I know the facts but I cannot make up my mind
to do anything about them"? Or a person may say, "I know
I ought not to feel as I do about him or her; it doesn't make
sense, but I do feel that way." What is needed is not more information, more facts, but an *aroused will*. The facts need to
be charged with concern, with emotion. Knowledge must be
shot through with dynamics, urgency and zeal. It is the easiest
thing in the world to admit you are wrong and to let it rest
there. Man is perhaps more a feeling creature than a thinking
creature. To know and to feel is to do. As long as my knowledge is untouched by concern, I have no stake in what the
knowledge reveals.

27.

THERE is a story in Buddhist writings concerning a certain
village whose population was being destroyed by the periodic
attacks of a cobra. At length, a holy man came to the village;
the plight of the people was made known to him. Immediately,
he sought the snake, to urge him to discontinue his destruction.
The snake agreed to leave the villagers alone. Days passed;
the villagers discovered that the snake was no longer danger-

ous. The word went from person to person: "The cobra does not bite any more. Something has happened to the cobra. The cobra does not bite any more." Almost overnight the attitude of everyone changed. The fear of the cobra disappeared and, in its place, there developed a daring boldness. All sorts of tricks were played on the cobra; his tail was pulled, water was thrown on him, little children threw sticks and bits of stone at him. There was no attempt to take his life by any direct means, only a great number of petty annoyances and cruelties which, when added up, rendered the snake's existence increasingly perilous. He was nearly dead when the holy man came back through the village. With great bitterness, the cobra implored, "I did as you commanded me; I stopped striking the villagers and now see what they have done to me. What must I do?" The holy man said in effect, "You did not obey me fully. It is true that I told you not to bite the people, but I did not tell you not to *hiss* at them." There must always remain as a part of the total equipment for survival at least the psychology of threat as a weapon of defense. All of this is a part of the problem of violence in life. It is curious how we do not even respect the person who does not seem able to affirm his right to be. There is an essential dignity in human life, yes, in all of life, that must somehow be asserted from within, or else life is stripped of any true significance. In religious terms, this essential dignity is the basis of reverence and is the symbol of the divine in life.

28.

THERE is a strange irony in the usual salutation, "Merry Christmas," when most of the people on this planet are thrown back upon themselves for food which they do not possess, for resources that have long since been exhausted, and for vitality which has already run its course. Nevertheless, the inescapable fact remains that Christmas symbolizes hope even at a moment when hope seems utterly fantastic. The raw materials of the Christmas mood are a newborn baby, a family, friendly animals, and labor. An endless process of births is the perpetual answer of life to the fact of death. It says that life keeps coming on, keeps seeking to fulfill itself, keeps affirming the margin of hope in the presence of desolation, pestilence and despair. It is not an accident that the birth rate seems always to increase during times of war, when the formal processes of man are engaged in the destruction of others. Welling up out of the depths of vast vitality, there is something at work that is more authentic than the formal discursive design of the human mind. As long as this is true ultimately, despair about the human race is groundless.

29.

IN an article in *The Atlantic Monthly*, Professor Toynbee has suggested the very real possibility that, if we are so foolish as to destroy our entire civilization and our own lives, then the creator of life could very easily make an ideal culture out of the ant. It is a most sobering thought. Again and again the human race has behaved as if it has some kind of monopoly on survival—and survival on its own terms, at that. The Church tends to foster this same notion. All the days of my life, I have heard men say that God is absolutely dependent upon the Church to spearhead His will and establish His true purposes among men; if the Church fails, God is exhausted, and there is no other means at His disposal. This seems to be essentially unsound; even men are more resourceful than that. Once upon a time, John remarked that if men were silent, then even the rocks would cry aloud. Men may grow and develop into more whole and complete beings, spreading all of life with a glory that springs out of an increasing understanding of the meaning and the possibilities of life; or they may become more and more involved in their own devices, petty dreams, and unworthy ends until, at last, the very processes which they have set in motion blot them from the earth. If this should happen, or if it should not, it must be remembered always that God is infinitely more resourceful and creative than any expression of life, however profound and exceptional that expression of life may be.

30.

ARE you tired or world-weary? There seems to be a mood of fatigue that pervades the life of modern man. Very often the weariness, the fatigue, reveals itself only in the monotony of activities, and the rapid increase in their tempo. So precisely does this seem to be the case that, the more physically exhausted we become, the more involved are we in additional activities. Years ago I heard a most vivid description of hell from the lips of an old minister who, in truth, was a consummate artist. Hell was not described in terms of fire and brimstone, but rather was it depicted as a place where each person was compelled to do for eternity that thing, the doing of which caused him to be in hell in the first place. The two things against which this minister was preaching were dancing and the playing of cards. Therefore he pictured a beautifully decorated ballroom floor filled with many dancing couples. They were not dancing for recreation or stimulation, and they were forced to dance forever and ever and with the same partner. Further, he dramatized the tired, wearied look on their faces; but the only manifestation in their movements was a feverishness in the tempo, the idea being that if the tempo were increased and increased, a point would be reached in which the body would snap and collapse; wonderful, blissful collapse would bring release. Not so in eternity, said the preacher. The analogy is an apt one in certain aspects. We are all of us deeply frightened and are trying to run away, only to discover that there is no place to go, there is no hiding place. We are afraid of a fearful depression in which, even more disastrously than before, we shall be reduced to penury and shame. We are afraid of the future because there looms on the horizon the visitation, upon us and our children, of the terror and the madness that we sent upon the Japanese at Hiroshima. To paraphrase our late President's remarks, we are afraid of fear. All of this results in the undermining of energy and the drying up of our resources for living as simple human beings. Hence we are tired all the time, world-weary, and there is little health in us. The old-fashioned word is needed. We may not be able to prevent the world from rushing into a destruction that will engulf all of us, we may not be able to stop the "warmongers" in Washington or Moscow, we may not be able to guarantee, in the slightest measure, our own security or the security of our children (Of course, I think we may); but one thing we can and must do is to find sources of strength and renewal for our own spirits, lest we perish.

31.

THERE seems to be a basic distinction between Fate and Destiny, particularly as touching human life. Again and again, we are startled by some incident that takes place without warning, apparently without cause and unmerited. The blow falls upon the innocent victim (But who is innocent?), the train jumps the rail, the accident happens and we are shocked, stunned or horrified. The word "accident," as it is commonly used, covers those experiences or events that appear without pattern outside a framework of order. All great religions have reckoned with this fact of life. Christianity suggests that nothing takes place outside of the will of God; and yet, there is the notion that large areas of life are under the control of the powers of darkness and therefore may be regarded as a kind of "lunatic fringe," capricious, evil and unmoral. The logic of such a position is that the events of a man's life may not be related to the quality of his character. "The people on whom the tower of Siloam fell, were they more guilty than the others on whom the tower did not fall?" asks Jesus. In the Moslem faith the word for this aspect of experience is "Kismet." Here it seems to be related to sin, as it is in the notion of Karma in certain of the great religions of the Orient. The man in the street recognizes the experience by calling it by the anonymous term "number." "He did not die because his number was not up." Thornton Wilder raised to the dimension of creative art a discussion of this problem in *The Bridge of San Luis Rey*. The fact is that, into all of our lives, things enter unannounced, unpredicted, often unprecedented. They change the whole structure of our living. They come alike to the poor and the rich, the "good" and the "bad," the guilty and the innocent, often leaving terror and desolation in their wake. Men call them Fate because they seem to fall by chance, by accident and without meaning and purpose. There is no outer protection against them and there is no escape. The unique thing here is the feeling of innocence which makes the notion of Fate carry with it that which is heartless and utterly impersonal. Destiny is a different matter. It is what a man does with his Fate.

32.

IT may seem to be splitting hairs to say that Destiny is what a man does with his fate. Fate is given; Destiny is won. Fate is the raw materials of experience. They come uninvited and often unanticipated. Destiny is what a man does with these raw materials. A man participates in his fate almost as a spectator or perhaps as a victim; he does not call the tunes. It is important to make clear that this is only an aspect of human experience. To ignore the margin of experience that seems to be unresponsive to any private will or desire is disastrous. To ascribe responsibility for all the things that happen to one to some kind of fate is equally disastrous. It is quite reasonable to say that there are forces in life that are set in motion by something beyond the power of man to comprehend or control. The purpose of such forces, their significance, what it is that they finally mean for human life, only God knows. The point at which they touch us or affect us cannot be fully understood. Why they affect us as they do, what they mean in themselves, we do not know. Sometimes they seem like trial and error, like accidents, like blind erratic power that is without conscience or consciousness, only a gross aliveness. To say that those forces are evil or good presupposes a knowledge of ends which we do not have. The point at which they affect our lives determines whether we call them good or evil. This is a private judgment that we pass upon a segment of our primary contact with the forces of life. Out of this contact we build our destiny. We determine what we shall do with our circumstances. It is here that religion makes one of its most important contributions to life. It is a resource that provides strength, stability and confidence as one works at one's destiny. It gives assurance of a God who shares in the issue and whose everlasting arms are always there.

> I know not where His islands lift
> Their fronded palms in air.
> I only know I cannot drift
> Beyond His love and care.

33.

THE mystic is forced to deal with social relations because, in his effort to achieve the good, he finds that he must be responsive to human need by which he is surrounded, particularly the kind of human need in which the sufferers are victims of circumstances over which, as individuals, they have no control; circumstances that are not responsive to the exercise of an individual will, however good and however perfect. This brings up for discussion the question of service. Canon Kirk writes, "Disinterested service is the only service that is serviceable." Now, what is disinterested service? Kirk further defines selfishness as "a lack of due regard to the well-being of others" and unselfishness as "the payment of due regard to the well-being of others." It would seem to me that disinterested service is a kind of service in which the person served is not a means to some end in which he does not share and participate directly. There are at least two levels of disinterestedness. In one, the individual is free from exploiting the need of others for purely narrow interest or gratification. An American novelist of the last century puts it this way: "No man may say I have smiled on him in order to use him, or called him my friend that I may make him do for me the work of a servant." In a second level of service, the individual would be interested in relieving human need, because he sees it, in some definite sense, crowding out of the life of others the possibility of developing those qualities of interior graces that will bring them into immediate candidacy for the vision of God. It is in this latter sense that we come upon the mandatory *raison d'être* of the mystic's interest in social change and in social action.

34.

MILLIONS of words have been written and spoken about the meaning of brotherhood in the world. Even the most careful observation reveals that there is something that misses fire, that is essentially inadequate in the usual brotherhood approach to human relations. Of course it is easy to say that the difficulty is in the fact that men who talk glibly about brotherhood are hypocrites and pretenders. Such judgments are apt to be superficial and needlessly cynical. It may be even safe to say that the purveyors of brotherhood are honest, sincere, genuine and devout. Nevertheless, the fact remains that even within organizations or institutions that are essentially built upon the brotherhood notion, the climate in which the individuals function, within and without, is decidedly unbrotherly. The difficulty seems to be in the fact that the concept of brotherhood is regarded as an essentially external relationship between human beings. It is therefore mechanical in character and is concerned with the externals of human behavior. The conventional approach to the meaning of brotherhood is comparable to the speech of the orator who places his emotions on the outside of the words that he uses and gives the general effect of being phonographic and mechanical. He reminds one of a record that is being played. The point is that the approach to the experience of brotherhood should be from the point of view of origin rather than from the point of view of the external relationships between a series of individuals. It is for this reason that religion approaches the question of brotherhood from the assumption that God is the common father of mankind. The center of focus is on the unity of life guaranteed by the identity of source. The thing that is propelling and mandatory in the practice of brotherhood is deep within the individual human being, and is not conditioned by the point of view, predicament, or plight of the individual. All men on this basis are intrinsically worthful as brothers because of the fact of origin rather than of the subsequent condition of life. Each man then stands in immediate candidacy for the activated feeling of brotherliness toward every other man. The mood of brotherliness, therefore, is not merely created by conformity to ethics, morality or value judgments, but is grounded in a gross awareness of the life process itself. When this awareness is heightened to the point that it becomes the formal basis of operation for the individual, that which men are in seed, they become in deed.

35.

ALL of us are sometimes overwhelmed by the smallness of our own lives, the complete tyranny of the details in which we are endlessly involved. There was a time when men thought that our earth was the center of everything and that even the sun revolved daily around it. After years of acceptance, this theory was rejected in favor of a more fruitful one, which made the sun the center of a system which bears its name, and the earth a small planet, a part of a great celestial host. Later, the earth was defined as a mere speck of stardust whirling mathematically through space. This change in theory concerning the earth has had a profound effect upon man's thought of himself. Significance must be redefined in terms more useful than those of space occupancy. When one considers that he lives only in the western half of the tiny speck of stardust, in the northern part of the western half of that tiny speck of stardust, the space we occupy is well nigh a vanishing quantity. All of this means that in addition to my own intrinsic worth, I must find some movement or cause or purpose that is more significant than my own life. I must find something that gives some radical test for all that is highest and best in me. This radical test must be as inclusive as possible, that one part of me shall not be betrayed by some other part of me. Otherwise, I may find myself involved in a series of commitments which tend to neutralize one another, thus rendering my life ineffective. This I must watch. In my relationship with people, with organizations of whatever character, with things, I must be working from one center, my concept of the highest. In the language of psychology, it is being an integrated, adjusted person; in the language of the meaning of culture, it is being a civilized, cultivated person. All of them say that at a man's center, he is not divided but he operates from a basis of inner certainty which gives meaning and clarity to whatever he does, however weak and feeble his achievement may be.

36.

I watched him for a long time. He was so busily engaged in his task that he did not notice my approach until he heard my voice. Then he raised himself erect with all the slow dignity of a man who had exhausted the cup of haste to the very dregs. He was an old man—as I discovered before our conversation was over, a full eighty-one years. Further talk between us revealed that he was planting a small grove of pecan trees. The little treelets were not more than two and a half or three feet in height. My curiosity was unbounded.

"Why did you not select larger trees so as to increase the possibility of your living to see them bear at least one cup of nuts?"

He fixed his eyes directly on my face, with no particular point of focus, but with a gaze that took in the totality of my features. Finally he said, "These small trees are cheaper and I have very little money."

"So you do not expect to live to see the trees reach sufficient maturity to bear fruit?"

"No, but is that important? All my life I have eaten fruit from trees that I did not plant, why should I not plant trees to bear fruit for those who may enjoy them long after I am gone? Besides, the man who plants because he will reap the harvest has no faith in life."

Years have passed since that sunny afternoon in LaGrange, Georgia, when those words were said. Again and again, the thought has come back to me, "Besides, the man who plants because he will reap the harvest has no faith in life." The fact

is that much of life is made up of reaping where we have not
sown and planting where we shall never reap. And yet that is
not all the story. There is a reaping of precisely what we have
sown, with the extra thrown in, guaranteed by the laws of
growth. Thus the insight from the scriptures: "Be not de-
ceived, God is not mocked, for whatsoever a man soweth that
shall he also reap." The good and the not-good alike. All of
life is a planting and a harvesting. No man gathers merely the
crop that he himself has planted. This is another dimension of
the brotherhood of man.

37.

AGAIN and again, in the course of the history of nations and
individuals, a single event becomes the critical point by which
the life or death of vast issues is determined. It is impossible
to know of what any event is prophetic and how many strands
of destiny are caught in a single pattern that is woven before
our very eyes. A chance word overheard by a passerby may
alter the entire structure of one's subsequent days. An impression made upon the mind of a growing child by some nameless
person, who crossed his path and disappeared, may be the
motif that shapes the fate of millions of people years after,
when the child has become a leader of men strategically placed
at a fateful crossroads in the history of a people. It is impossible
to know when a moment is *the* moment, when an act is *the*
act, when an issue is *the* issue. In 165 B.C. a Jewish leader,
Judas Maccabeus, with or without a sense of destiny, spear-

headed the funded hopes and dreams and dedicated passions of Israel, and flung them triumphantly in the face of the legions of Antiochus Epiphanes (in a decisive battle that) unravelling a thread out of which the patterns of Christianity and Mohammedanism were woven. It is well within the mark to say that, if that for which Judas Maccabeus stood had been defeated, it is not unreasonable to assume that Judaism would have perished; and without Judaism there would have been no Christianity and no Mohammedanism. The human family would have been easily involved indefinitely in pouring out its votive offerings before altars of idolatry, stark and meaningless, yielding no hope and no response. It is in celebration of this event of what may be regarded as unconscious destiny that the Feast of Lights is commemorated for eight days in December in countless Jewish homes all over the world. A single event in history—a man who refuses to renounce his faith either by default or in defeat—becomes, in the circling wisdom of a Providence, rich in variety and creativity, the gate through which have marched hundreds of generations of men to a life abundant and a hope undimmed.

38.

ONE day Jesus told a parable about a man out of whom a devil had been cast. When the job had been completed, he felt perfectly safe and secure. He may have said to himself, "Now, that is done. He is gone and my house is at peace. I shall buy new furnishings, put up fresh curtains, and give to the entire place a new look." This was done. Late in the afternoon, largely by force of habit, the devil that had been evicted decided to walk down by his old home to see what had transpired in the meanwhile. To his amazement he found everything clean, fresh and rearranged, but empty of occupancy. With a flash of insight, he sized up the situation, called friends and cronies, and, together with them, he re-established himself in his old setting. Jesus adds, "And the last state of the man was worse than the first." The story illustrated a profound truth about the nature of life. That which is left untended seems to disintegrate. Effort does not need to be exercised in order to accomplish such an end. Weeks ago, I took all the weeds and grass out of my garden, planted some flowers. Time passed without my paying much attention to the garden. In a manner almost uncanny, grass appeared all around the flowers, wrapping its roots around the roots of each plant. The assumption that, because a thing is right or good, it will take care of itself without anything else being done, is false. There seems to be present in life a dramatic principle that is ever alert to choke off, to strangle, the constructively creative. Those persons who are working on behalf of the avowedly evil in life recognize this fact and seek to utilize it to the full. Usually they proceed on the basis of a plan, or structure of orderliness, which harnesses all available resources to the ends which they seek. In a sense there is a recognition of the fact that the presuppositions in life are against them and they must make up for this by extra effort and concentration. The good must be worked at, must be concentrated upon, if it is to prevail in any short-time intervals. Religion assumes that, ultimately, the universe itself will not sustain the evil, but it does not assume that evil will not triumph in the short range. It is not enough to evict the devil; but something else must be put in his place and maintained there, or else he returns, refreshed and recharged, to deliver us over to a greater tyranny.

39.

THE quest for freedom looms larger and larger on the horizon of modern man. It is brought more sharply into focus than ever before, perhaps because of the ever tightening grip of the machine. Vast areas of life that once were fashioned and operated by a kind of rough creativity on the part of man are now completely routinized by the machine. Leisure is becoming more and more inescapable and compulsory. Because it is compulsory, leisure is apt to be tyrannical and boring. To be able to win a span of leisure, by juggling one's responsibilities and choosing here and rejecting there, yields a certain fundamental sense of freedom for the individual. Basically, freedom is a sense of alternatives. Where there is no alternative, there is no freedom. It needs the privilege of option. Note that I say the *privilege* of option. The option need not be taken, for it may often be sufficient to know that one has an option. It is this sense of alternative that is freedom. If I had no alternative, then I could not be free. Therefore, if my freedom were perfect, absolute, it would be equivalent to slavery. Wherever human beings are denied the exercise of option, they are not free. This is confined to no particular aspect of life but is quite inclusive. "You shall know the truth and the truth shall make you free." The spirit of truth and the spirit of freedom are the same, for the truth is found only in the presence of alternatives. At long last it may be terribly accurate that paradox is the test of reality.

40.

PARADOXICAL as it seems, patience is an important technique for accomplishing difficult tasks, even in matters having to do with social change. Several years ago, I spent three wintry days visiting Dalhousie University in Nova Scotia. A young medical student drove me in his car to keep various appointments. I was impressed with the fact that, despite the huge snow drifts, he refused to use chains. There was quite a ceremony every time he started out. First, he would let his clutch out slowly, applying the gas very gently as he chanted, "Even a little energy applied directly to an object, however large, will move it, if steadily applied and given sufficient time to work." Not once during our experience was his car stalled in the snow. Of course, he knew how to wait. Waiting was not inactivity; it was not resignation; it was a dynamic process, what Otto calls "the numinous silence of waiting." Sometimes I think that patience is one of the great characteristics that distinguishes God from man. God knows how to wait, dynamically; everybody else is in a hurry. Some things cannot be forced but they must unfold, sending their tendrils deep into the heart of life, gathering strength and power with the unfolding days.

This is manifestly a dangerous doctrine because it suggests that men must accept evil, exploitation, poverty, etc., confident that in due time things will come around all right. There are situations that must be changed, must be blasted out, there is a place for radical surgery. Patience, in the last analysis, is only partially concerned with time, with waiting; it includes also the quality of relentlessness, ceaselessness and constancy. It is a mood of deliberate calm that is the distilled result of confidence. One works at the task intensely even as one realizes that to become impatient is to yield the decision to the adversary. Live life seriously; it is a mistake to take it seriously.

41.

THE question of the Christian's attitude toward the world is of primary importance. It is obvious that the Christian undertakes to live each day on the basis of an idealism and a conviction that is at variance with the general pattern of society. He is in the world sharing fundamentally in its life. What must be his attitude toward it? He may try to ignore the world, living as if he were not really in the world. The result of this may lead to a mood of withdrawal and an increasing nonparticipation. This means that the weight of his influence will not be registered on behalf of the things in which he believes and about which he is under obligation to be concerned. Or he may endeavor to keep from being affected by the world, in the world but not affected by it. This results in a hardness and insensitiveness or even downright indifference. One may say that he is so sensitive to human needs, for instance, that he cannot afford to run the risk of exposure to suffering. Such an exposure may very easily result in complete mental collapse. There are many people who feel that they cannot possibly endure the thought of the great privation and anguish in the world without disintegration. Such persons will gladly give money to others to make the direct contact with suffering and they will be content with the readings of reports. Or, again, one may decide that all of the experiences of life are raw materials out of which the Christian is to build the New Jerusalem under God. Such a person will not shrink from the world, but will work in it with courage and high purpose, with the full consciousness that this is God's world.

42.

THERE is a general notion abroad that the wise man accepts the universe, accepts life. The notion is sound because it reveals a direct understanding of the most elementary fact of life, namely, that the universe is here and we are in it. This does not mean that we should not have an attitude toward it, nor that we should not use it as raw material for building our dreams. It does mean that I and every other man must accept the fact of our existence in a world, the basic structure of which we did not in any way create or determine. In this acceptance there should be no fear, but a quiet confidence in the reliability of life. "The everlasting arms sustain us," is the language used by the Psalmist. This I can depend upon. I am not cut adrift in the universe; I am intimately a part of a sure, closely knit structure. And I am not alone. This fact is the naked insight that feeds the impulse to prayer wherever it appears. The whispered, stammering incoherence of the panic stricken, the deep exhaltation of the mystic, the lisping of the child struggling with the simple words of "Now I lay me down to sleep," the sigh of relief when some tragic moment has passed without the terrible consequence, all these and much, much more are variations on the theme, I am not alone. Whitehead is most suggestive when he says that religion is what a man does with his solitariness. It is here that he discovers his God and begins his quest for God among the ways of men and in the life of a great and ever fascinating world.

43.

SOME years ago, Mahatma Gandhi wrote a letter to Muriel Lester to encourage her in her work on behalf of India's freedom. An excerpt from this letter said, "Speak the truth, without fear and without exaggeration, and see everyone whose work is relative to your purpose. You are in God's work, so you need not fear men's scorn. If they listen to your requests, and grant them, you will be satisfied. If they reject them, then you must make their rejection your strength." This quotation reveals much about the spiritual insights and understanding of Mr. Gandhi. Very often the man of deep conviction or of singleness of mind acts as if he is in some profound sense completely autonomous and independent. Sometimes a person is so sure of the truth which is in his heart, so completely abandoned to the creative stirrings within him, that he does not think it is necessary to recognize the part that other people play in the fulfillment of the ends to which he is dedicated. It is so easy to expect God to perform the miracle merely because of the intense quality of our individual dedication. The truth which Mr. Gandhi suggested to Muriel Lester is abundantly illustrated in his own life. Without compromising his ideal, without relaxing his concern for the freedom of his people, he sought constantly to win to his cause the sympathetic interest and effective concern of all those whose work was related to the life of the Indian people. His record is replete with numerous conferences with viceroys, governors, and many others. The significant thing is that, in none of his contacts and conferences, would he appear as a beggar. It is a curious thing that when a man moves into action on the basis of a deep inner commitment, even though he may be seeking from the hands of others those things which they are in a position to grant, he does so as one who would enlist them in an enterprise rather than as one who seeks of them a favor. "Speak the truth [then] without fear and without exaggeration, and see everyone whose work is related to your purpose." There can be no substitute for the principle suggested here.

44.

Here is another man who brought to his life-task a deep and abiding passion. His basic equipment was a robust and virile physique capable of sustained endurance over time intervals of well nigh limitless duration. In addition he was possessed with a mind capable of vast concentration under circumstances of rare difficulty. Also he was given a religious heritage of authentic piety, which nurtured his spirit in the ways of simple spiritual truth and daring. With all of these, there was in him the holy hush of pure music that sensitized his whole being with endless harmonies and rich melodies that only the organ could make manifest in sound. At precisely the moment in his life when he was ready to make the offering of his many-sided creativity and disciplines to the needs of his fellows, he forsook the accepted paths and sallied forth to a part of the world which was easily regarded as a living grave for men of his race and talents. He went to Africa. And to what end? He was caught in the struggle of a great urgency to make of his life a living and skilled atonement for the sins of white men in that great continent. What an impossible undertaking! As if one man in a thousand lifetimes could heal the wounds and restore the balance that ruthlessness, greed and exploitation had perpetrated. The tremendous arrogance of his daring was matched only by the intensity of his devotion and the astonishing character of his abilities and preparation. The phrase "reverence for life" has become identified with him in Western thought. It came to him as a flash of blinding light, as he wrestled with the meaning of life in the midst of a thousand tasks in his ministry of healing among the sick and diseased of body and mind on the banks of the Ogowe River. By some, he is regarded as a pantheist moving under the banner of a Christianity in which he does not believe; to others, he is a ball of fire attacking the wooden scaffolding of a precious dogma; to still others, he is a symbol of all that is best in a culture and civilization decadent with materialism and greed. But to all who contemplate his life against the background of hopelessness and despair which besets our age, Albert Schweitzer is a dramatic revelation of the witness to truth made manifest when a man of large powers places himself, in utter devotion, in the hands of the living God, in a living world, among living men.

45.

I knew a man who was like one of the ancient prophets. There was something of the eternal in the rolling sound of his majestic voice. It conjured up forgotten judgments and an almost terrible sense of the littleness of men in the vast panorama of the collective destiny of man. There was something dazzling about the burning brilliance of his mind. Moments there were, when one listened to his words, that seemed to be all light, and all the little dark caverns of one's prejudices and fears melted away in their unearthly radiance. Caught up in such an experience, all separateness of religion, culture and nationality seemed strangely unreal and far removed. He was the authentic embodiment of a dream, the ancient dream of a homeland for Israel, the wanderer upon the face of the earth. He lived it, talked it, felt it and thought it until at last the magic of its power became to many what it was to him. There is always a nostalgic uneasiness that creeps over one as he is brought face to face with a man possessed by the homeland dream. It arouses forgotten memories of the abandoned securities of one's child-hood and youth. It gives one a sense of passing but burning shame that what one takes for granted as a birthright is too lightly held and too loosely regarded. Often it inspires a fresh sense of gratitude to unknown pioneers and pilgrims into whose heritage one has come with little knowledge of what struggles entered into its making. Despite all of this, he gather-ed into the sweep of his concern the tragic plight of all victims of injustice and hate. With them he made common cause, often mingling his tremendous powers with the dumb inar-ticulate stirring of those whose misery could only be known to the infinite tenderness of a suffering God. And now he is dead. That Voice is stilled. The champion lays down his shield, and all the tools made useful in the sustained encounter with evil are laid aside. It is not difficult to believe that, in years to come, when some daring dreamer sees a deeper meaning and a greater glory in an ancient faith and calls men to walk therein, he will feel a strange new courage feeding the hidden fires of his dreams; when some gaping wrong cries aloud for righting, and power comes to those who dare to pick up the cudgel; when some uprooted peoples find the banked fires of their homeland-longing blaze suddenly into tremendous conflagration, there will be moving across the horizon of men's minds the spirit to which this great man of Israel gave himself in such unyielding devotion. And some there will be who will not be loath to name it as that of which Rabbi Stephen Wise was the living embodiment.

II

A Sense of Self

THERE must be also a developed sense of self. This is important because it is only on such a basis that the dignity of man, the individual, can be restored. There must be some understanding of what it is that men seek and of the varied means they use in order to find. Stripped to the literal substance of ourselves, what is it that we want and need in order to be worthful persons in our own sight? The assumption of democracy, that the quality of infinite worth is the priceless ingredient in human life and relations, must be examined and re-emphasized.

1.

THE quest for stability is pursued against a background of threatening confusion and impelled by a desire for personal morale. Its achievement results in a profound *sense of self*. It is important, therefore, to find out what a *sense of self* may mean as the object of our search. In the first place, one's personal stability depends on his relationships with others. For, in order to answer the question, "Who am I?" the individual must go on to ask, "To whom, to what do I belong?" This primary sense of belonging, of counting, of participating in situations, of sharing with the group, is the basis of all personal stability. And from it is derived the true *sense of self*. We are all related either positively or negatively to some immediate social unit which provides the other-than-self reference which in turn undergirds the sense of self. Such a primary group confers *persona* upon the individual; it fashions and fortifies the character structure. It is so important that most of our choices, decisions and actions are taken in the light of their bearing upon our relationship with the group or groups that give to us dignity, self-respect, status, a sense of self. Whenever I ask myself, "What do I wish—what do I want to do?" I am almost sure to raise the broader question, "How will this affect my standing with others?" For experience tells us that disapproval and criticisms are likely to emasculate or even to annihilate our sense of self and so to strip us of all personal significance. At such moments, if we can find a strong personality to lean to, we fasten upon him with such utter dependence that we become in important ways his reflection. Sometimes, after a bitter humiliation, when we so greatly need help for our healing, for being made whole again, we are introduced to a personality who brings us what we need and stays with us, until slowly, and often with great pain, we are able to stand on our own feet once more. And so we regain personal stability. Another question that we instinctively ask is, "What am I?" The answer rests in part with the quality of our achievements—our ability to express ourselves in effective action. Yet no one's deeds offer an adequate account of his entire personality. There is always a margin of self not quite involved in whatever he may be thinking, saying or doing at any particular moment. For each person is both a *participant* and a *spectator*. No self-expression can be perfectly complete.

2.

For every man, there is a necessity to establish as securely as possible the lines along which he proposes to live his life. In developing his life's working paper, he must take into account many factors, in his reaction to which he may seem to throw them out of line with their true significance. As a man, he did not happen. He was born, he has a name, he has forbears, he is the product of a particular culture, he has a mother tongue, he belongs to a nation, he is born into some kind of faith. In addition to all of these, he exists, in some curious way, as a person independent of all other facts. There is an intensely private world, all his own; it is intimate, exclusive, sealed. The life working paper of the individual is made up of a creative synthesis of what the man is in all his parts and how he reacts to the living processes. It is wide of the mark to say that a man's working paper is ever wrong; it may not be fruitful, it may be negative, but it is never wrong. For such a judgment would imply that the synthesis is guaranteed to be of a certain kind, of a specific character, resulting in a foreordained end. It can never be determined just what a man will fashion. Two men may be born of the same parents, grow up in the same environment, be steeped in the same culture and inspired by the same faith. Close or even cursory observation may reveal that each has fashioned a life working paper so unique that different roads are taken, and each day the two men grow farther and farther apart. Or it may be that they move along precisely parallel lines that never meet. Always, then, there is the miracle of the working paper. Wherever there appears in human history a personality whose story is available and whose reach extends far in all directions, the question of his working paper is as crucial as is the significance of his life. We want to know what were the lines along which he decided to live his life. How did he relate himself to the central issues of his time? What were the questions which he had to answer? Was he under some necessity to give a universal character to his most private experience?

3.

A father was trying to put into words the basic difference between his two children. At length he said, "The best way I can describe it is to put it this way: when they were babies, one of them always crawled around an object that blocked the path; while the other one always tried to push it out of the way." Many times since, the picture has come before me. It is not a poor description of two basic techniques in human relations. There are those who seem always to steer their course around opposition, around those persons or positions that stand in the path before them. It seems never to occur to them to try to remove the obstacle. Sometimes the reason is that it is not worth the effort, because the greatest possible economy must be exercised in getting to the goal. No undue risks must be run that may involve one in the possibility of being stopped altogether. There are times when to crawl around the block is the result of a decision based upon a careful analysis of the character of the opposition. It represents the only solution to the difficulty. In a sense, it is a safety first device. A fine line must be drawn between a deliberate technique of action such as has been described and a bias in temperament. There are temperaments that crawl around obstacles—a simple behavior pattern, the resultant of glands and early conditioning. This is what the father said in fact about one of his children. The other method is to knock all opposition out of the way. One of the wisest things a teacher told me once was: "It is all right to close some doors but never slam them." There is a certain strength in the method which pushes things out of the way so as to keep the track clear as one goes along. Often the threat to push obstacles aside causes them to step aside or to melt away. But the assumption that all obstacles can be handled in that manner is obviously not correct. Sometimes a decision has to be made—

to go around the obstacle or to be destroyed by the obstacle. The matter of timing is crucial. Some things can be removed only by allowing them to *soak*. To know the difference in techniques demanded is a kind of wisdom that cannot be easily won. It is the wisdom of God.

4.

IT is small wonder that all religions that are ethically sensitive place a great emphasis upon the corrosive effects of pride upon the human spirit. There is something very subtle about pride and arrogance of spirit. Often it assumes the garb of utter self-lessness and humility. It expresses itself in pointed and dramatic self-effacement and very articulate modesty. There is often stark pride in calling attention to one's willingness always to humble oneself, to take the back seat, to accept the menial task. The most obvious basis for pride is in the act of comparing one's deeds with the deeds of others, one's achievements with the work of others. In any field of endeavor or activity, this tendency is apparent. It may be found in the comments of a parent about some other person's child, some remark made by a wife about husbands in general or a husband in particular. The idea is effectively personalized in the story which Jesus tells of the two men who went up in the temple to pray. One man said that he thanked God that he was not as other men, he paid his vows, he prayed regularly. He paused in the midst of his other duties to go into the temple to let God know how good he was. The other man, an acknowledged sinner, dared not lift his countenance to look aloft but beat at his breast asking God to be merciful to him a sinner. There is no form of pride that is quite so devastating as pride of the man who is sure that he is not victimized by pride. It is for this reason that the man who has the pride of self-righteousness can be so hard and unyielding in dealing with others, that he can sacrifice often such feelings as tenderness, sympathy, even love, in carrying out the ruthless insistence of his autorighteous urges. The possibility of error is regarded by him as a betrayal. It must always be remembered that the ideal is the only thing, the only standard by which one's achievements must be measured. It is fatal to measure them by the work of another man's hand or by another's end results. To state this in terms of religious experience, a vivid sense of the judgment of God is the only antidote to pride. That is why the holiest man is ever the one who *honestly* regards himself as the chief of sinners. Whatever men may think of us, however proud, righteous and decent we may be, in the eyes of God we are in some profound sense, sinners.

5.

Is this a world with moral meaning at the center? This is the primary question. It must be answered before other questions can even be asked. True, it can never be answered with proof and finality, but some answer must be given on the level of faith. In history, men have often tried to side-step facing the question by saying, "We can never know"; but it cannot be side-stepped. To decide not to decide, is to decide against. The negation of inactivity is just as potent as the emphatic vocal "No!" Only when one has said "Yes," or has said "No," or has given what amounts to "No" by saying nothing—only then can one face the other basic problems: since there is meaning, what is the nature of that meaning? or since there is no meaning, how shall we act in accordance with this terrible negative? Life affirmation is not possible unless we summon enough courage to make the first basic act of faith: "I believe that there is moral meaning at the center of life!" Unfortunately, it is easily possible—much too easily possible—to make this affirmation with gusto and enthusiasm without really meaning it. Not that it is easy to be insincere, but that it is difficult really to mean it. This is simply because there is evidence on either side. We see the sordid and the tragic in life; we see the pain and suffering. This is evidence, we may say, against there being meaning at the center. Then we see beauty, truth, love and fulfillment, and we say, "This is evidence on behalf of meaning." And the evidence is always straining within us. In consequence, we may decide intellectually in favor of meaning, only to find our subconscious casting a dissenting ballot. Douglas Steere says most of us are not integrated selves but each of us is a whole committee of selves and decisions are made by majority vote. The result is vocal life affirmation, and active life negation. We are committed to meaning only in an equivocal way. Therefore, the great labor of life, after we have made the initial life affirmation, is to validate the decision in practice. After all, how can one believe that life has meaning, if his own life does not have meaning. No words, no matter how eloquently and enthusiastically uttered, can replace the expressiveness of action. Indeed, words become true when they are lived, and they become untrue when the living of them is neglected. We shall always be ambivalent, and our "Yes" will never have the total assent of our total wills. Our great labor is simply to bring active affirmation as close as possible to the vocal affirmation. All else is subsidiary.

6.

"Nothing fails like success" is a quotation that reverses the usual saying, "Nothing succeeds like success." The latter is based upon the assumption that success tends to snowball, to reproduce itself in the minds of people, to inspire by sheer contagion. There is certainly an element of accuracy in the observation. Jesus gives expression to the same idea in the statement, "To him that hath, some shall be given, but from him that hath not, even that which he seems to have shall be taken away." A queer turn of events, to be sure. And yet it is grounded in an important aspect of human experience. Usually, if a man has money, he can borrow money. If he has a job he can find a job. If he has friends, he can get more friends. It may be that the fact of being in no great need of a thing because of an abundance of it, gives to the individual a confidence, a sense of authority and power, that creates a vacuum, drawing to him more of the same. The matter can be more easily understood when it relates to the attitude taken toward institutions, movements or organizations. The explanation is in terms of crowd psychology or the reappearance of the herd instincts in a given situation. The more people who are interested, the more the word spreads. The more the word spreads, the greater is apt to be the overall response. The saying, "Nothing fails like success," however, calls attention to an oft overlooked insight. The particular situation is viewed from the inside rather than the outside. The quotation raises the question of the effect of success upon the person or the object that is succeeding. One of the best summaries of this point of view is found in a little poem written by Glenn Ward Dresbach:

> There is defeat where death gives anodyne
> And all desires of the battle wane
> In deep forgetfulness, and the one slain
> Lies with his face turned toward the firing-line.
> There is defeat where flesh fails the design
> Of Spirit, and the groping, tortured brain
> Sees glories lost it cannot win again.
> And wears itself out like effect of wine.
> But no defeat is quite so imminent
> To common ways as the defeat Success
> Turns into when it puts aside the dreams
> That made it be, and somehow, grows content
> With what it is, forever giving less
> Until it is not, and no longer seems.[1]

"Nothing fails like success" is a warning, calling attention to a peril that is apt to turn up in the highroad of achievement.

[1]"Defeat." Used by permission of the author.

7.

For a long time there was current, as a part of the folklore of a certain section of the country, the story that during the month of August the rattlesnake sheds his old skin and a new one takes its place. There may be an actual basis for this in the life history of the snake. But be that as it may. The folk account is that, during this period, the snake remains immobile and is blind. At the slightest movement near him, he strikes out in his blindness, directing his attack by the sense of sound. If some object touches his body, in his panic, he strikes the spot that has been touched, releasing into his own body the deadly poison which he carries in his fangs. The result is death—suicide. In some of its aspects, this is indeed a telling analogy. A sense of defenselessness—fear mounting to panic—striking out blindly—destroying oneself thereby. The phrase "loss of temper" is one of those combination of words descriptive of a total state of being. It means a dissipation of powers, a vital exhaustion. It is a blind striking at an object which often ends in deep injury, self-inflicted. Deep injury, because things are said, words are used, that can never be recalled or unuttered. How many times a man looks at the terrible work of his words, spoken in anger, and says, "I didn't really mean that; I lost my head." The injury to the other person is not the crucial matter here, important as that may be. For, after all, your words beat upon the outside of the other, and their damage of necessity is limited by that fact. The authentic damage is done to oneself. The dignity of the self has been outraged; a profound sense of shame and humiliation is present. This is no claim for repression and the complications resulting therefrom. But it is a recognition of the fact that to give oneself over to rage is self-destructive. There must be a recognition of responsibility for one's action. A "loss of temper" is a luxury that carries with it a heavy tax that may send one into acute bankruptcy. It is in order to suggest that in the living of one's life, it is deadly to possess and encourage the mood that is expressed in the folklore concerning the behavior of the rattlesnake during the month of August. The best place for your temper is at home in you. There, it gives you power, courage, vitality; on the rampage, it is a terror—especially to you!

8.

W E live our days on the basis of the options which we take. Despite the evidence to the contrary, each of us takes options on various things. The use of our time, for instance. Every person has twenty-four hours at his disposal. This period is divided into functional units—so many hours for sleeping, eating, working, etc. One person elects to give less to sleep, more to work, or less to work and more to recreation. What a man does with his twenty-four hours is in large part an indication of how he deals with his available options. How he deals with available options is determined in large part by what it is that he seeks to be, to become, or to do in life. The options may not be taken consciously. It is quite possible for a man to drift with the pressing demands of his environment, thereby letting his options be determined by circumstances. We have all had experiences of planning for definite things to be accomplished during a particular week or month, only to discover that the time passes and, for one reason or another, very little was accomplished. The reasons are all excellent but not crucial. Sometimes options go by default because of certain habits into which we drift. The habit of putting things off from one day to the next is to let one's options go by default. It means increasing entanglement and confusion. Of course, the taking of an option means the decision to do one thing rather than something else, which something else may be important to do. The thing that is not done is put off for some other time. This is not to be condemned; for it means that one lives quite deliberately on the basis of a discriminating plan. In the last analysis we tend to do the things that we really want to do. We plan for the things that are to us essential. This is true not only with reference to our time, our friends, but also our money. Most of us are poor, but even this is highly relative. Any examination of the way an individual spends his money will show that he uses it to do those things that reveal his philosophy of living. Here is a person who finds it convenient to spend $1.10 for a taxi to get to church in time for most of the service, but puts 10 cents in the collection plate. Another person spends several hundred dollars a year for clothes and premium recreation, but will give $3.00 to the community chest. One's entire life, which includes one's time, money, presence and vocation, is lived on the basis of the choice of options. The choice of options is determined by the philosophy of life which one has accepted as determinative. What one really seeks in life is strikingly revealed by the emphasis expressed in the options taken. The exercise of options does not always have a margin of freedom. It is true that the time may pass for what may be regarded as a live option. The well worn quotation from Shakespeare about the "tide in the affairs of men" is on the point. There are certain options available to us when we are young, as the beginning of life and all the world stretches out before us, boundless and unexplored. One of the most dramatic aspects of man's experience with options is the way in which the environment influences options. During a period of great social upheaval, when all the normal patterns of life are disturbed, options may be definitely reduced both in richness and in variety. During periods of war, options available are very few indeed for men and women within certain age brackets. Marriage has to be postponed or hastily entered into. Lifework or vocational possibilities are definitely curtailed or cut short completely. The environment closes in, reducing the possible options almost to zero. Sickness alters options as well. I knew a man who wanted to go as a teacher to China. The sudden death of his father forced him to take over a business so as to hold the family intact. For several years, he felt that he had missed his one great opportunity to be of service. An option was forced upon him against his plan and desires. It happened that the business was retailing shoes. He had observed that many of his customers complained because of bad-fitting shoes, even when the size was correct. After much experimentation, he designed two basic lasts that provided maximum comfort with no sacrifice in style. He lived to see many people made happier and easier to live with, at home and at work, because their feet were comfortable. The option that was forced upon him was turned to creative account even though his desired option was denied him. But there is one option that remains ever available—I can select the things *against* which I shall stand with my life and the things *for* which I shall stand. No one can prevent me there. I must deal with this basic and unalterable option directly or by default. To accept this responsibility is to alert oneself for the high adventure in living which God has vouchsafed for the children of men.

9.

A friend of mine was given an assignment in a class in dramatics. Each time she tried to read her selection aloud before the class, tears came and her strong emotional reaction made it impossible to go through with it. One day the teacher asked her to remain after class for a conference. The essence of the teacher's words to her was this: "You must read the selection before the class tomorrow. I understand what is happening to you and that is why I insist that you do this tomorrow. It is important that you realize that you must read this selection through, crying every step of the way, perhaps, if you expect to read it through without crying." A very wise teacher. There are experiences through which we must go, crying all the way, perhaps, if we are ever to go through them without crying, and to go through them without crying must be done. St. Francis of Assisi, in his youth, found it impossible to control his deep physical and emotional revulsion against leprosy. So acute was his reaction that he could not ever run the risk of looking at a leper. Shortly after he had made his first commitment to his Lord, he was riding down the road, when suddenly there appeared a leper. Instinctively, he turned his horse around and went galloping off in the opposite direction, his whole body bathed in nervous sweat. Then he realized what he was doing. Leprosy was one of the things he could not stand—as long as that was true, leprosy would be his jailer, his master. He turned around as abruptly as before, found the leper and, according to the story, remained with him, living intimately with him until every trace of his previous reaction had been mastered. Thus freed, he could be of tremendous service to the victims of the disease. You must go through some things, crying all the way, perhaps, if you are ever to live with them without crying. This is an important law of living. There are many experiences which we face that are completely overwhelming. As we see them, they are too terrible even to contemplate. And yet we must face them and deal with them directly. We chide ourselves because at first we tend to go to pieces. Go to pieces, then. Weep all the way through the first terrible impact, if need be. This may be the only way that you will ever be able to deal with the problem without emotional upheaval. To deal with it without emotional upheaval is necessary if you are ever going to be able to manage it at all. There can be no more significant personal resolution at the beginning of the New Year than this: I will face the problem I have been putting off because of too much fear, of too much tears, of too much resentment, even if it means crying all the way through, in order that I may deal with it without fear, tears, or resentment.

10.

THERE is a simple and inescapable dignity in working with one's hands. Men have always placed a high premium upon the ability to fashion, to create beautiful and/or useful things with one's hands. The hands become the living, sensitive instrument for the mind. First, there is the conception, the idea, the plan—then the technique, the method by which the conception may take form and visibility. Sometimes the conception is so elaborate or intricate that the time interval needed for its physical creation is very long. The exhilaration that comes from such work is the result of the effect in the mind and the spirit of brooding over the unfinished stuff of nature until it is shaped into the likeness of one's dreams. There is the high, free sense of creation, of seeing the unfolding of the act in tangible fact. The will to create seems to be basic in the structure of personality. It is the ground of procreation with all the glory and the wonder that attend it. When men are free, they take a simple pride in the work of their hands. Such work bears the distinctive mark of the creator and in a sense it becomes his signature. As society has become more complex and industrialized, the gulf between the created article and the creator has widened. In addition, work on any particular article in our civilization is a combination of many efforts so that the individual has little sense of actual participation in the act and in the making of the finished product. It is for this reason that the economic unit, money, has become a substitute for the sense of creation in work. Important as money is, it is a poor and inadequate substitute. There is no more critical problem facing our civilization than this, because it undermines the dignity of the individual at the point of his belonging to the social fabric. It is obvious that we cannot turn back the clock and once again have the simple economy that obtained when the worker shared responsibility in a total sense in the things he created through his labor. This means that some way must be found by which the worker can once more be identified with his creation. The problem is also tied up with the disposal of the objects created. However long we may be in working out this problem, each of us can develop, within the scope of his total experience, more little areas of specific work which will give to him a primary sense of deep expression. This is the authentic basis for hobbies of a certain kind. One of the antidotes for the loss of dignity in labor, as far as the particular individual is concerned, is the finding for oneself some tangible expression for the hands, for the mind, for the personality.

11.

In a sports article by Arthur Daley appearing in the *New York Times* there was a story about Durocher, the former manager of the Brooklyn Dodgers. It told of the days, some twenty years ago, when Durocher was playing for St. Paul in a game with Toledo. He directed some heated remarks at a certain Joe Kelly, who pretended to be very hard of hearing. Coming close to Durocher he said, "What did you say, runt?" Durocher repeated his remarks; whereupon Kelly said, "That's what I thought you said." There was silence—a dramatic, loaded silence—then Kelly swung. Durocher lost several teeth in the encounter. A certain Charles Stengel observed the incident and tucked it away in his mind for future reference. Years passed. One day, Durocher and Stengel were opposing managers in a big series. So critical was the situation that only cold deliberateness could be effective. Just before the crucial game of the series, Durocher walked past the dugout where Stengel sat. "Hey, Leo," called out Stengel, "who is your dentist these days?" Of course, Durocher lost his temper. A fight threatened but friends pulled them apart. All the afternoon, so the story goes, Durocher was upset. The one telling remark had done its perfect work so that he was completely at a disadvantage. Stengel knew precisely what to say to Durocher to make him lose his temper and thereby render him vulnerable. If a person knows what word he can use to address you so as to draw you off balance, he can always keep you at his mercy. The basis of one's inner togetherness, one's sense of inner authority, must never be at the mercy of factors in one's environment, however significant they may be. Nothing from outside a man can destroy him until he opens the door and lets it in. A friend was driving his family cross-country. He was determined to reach a certain city before stopping to rest, despite the fact that he was so sleepy he could hardly keep the car on the road. His wife's remonstrances were of no avail. There was a certain matter that could never be discussed without his getting angry. Quietly, she introduced this into the conversation. The reaction was instantaneous. He was awakened so completely that he drove into the city without apparent fatigue. Whatever determines how you feel on the inside controls in large part the destiny of your life.

12.

> The worry cow
> Would have lasted till now,
> If she hadn't lost her breath.
> But she thought her hay
> Wouldn't last all day,
> So she mooed herself to death.

THE apt little ditty puts its finger on one of the central disorders of our times. Of course, the obvious meaning of the lines has to do with the individual who tends always to cross bridges before he gets to them, to become exercised over the possible bad outcome of any and all events. There is a little of this in even the most balanced personality. Such a tendency appears as the outer rim of pessimism which dramatizes the central core of vitality in the so-called optimist. It is the mood of the "Yes, but" or the "All right, but on the other hand" individuals. It marches under the banner of "I am a realist" or "I always look facts in the face." Often the tendency becomes more apparent when there is some basic organic or functional difficulty as touching the matter of health. It may be the result of faulty diet. A friend of mine was talking with me about her rabbits. Her favorite rabbit was a beautiful female. One day she found that this rabbit had eaten two of her own babies. It was discovered that a certain mold had appeared in her feed with the effect that all the protein had been taken out of it. This caused the otherwise wonderful mother to become the worst possible enemy to her new young. Your worry may be rooted in faulty diet or poor gland functioning or some other form of physical unadjustment. It may be the result of something else that really has no bearing upon the problem before your mind. Most often, however, worry is a lack of confidence in life, in its purpose, in God. Faith in life, in God, is native to the human spirit. It cannot die as long as a man lives. It turns into pessimism, into depression, into anxiety, into worry, into drawn-out fear, but it will not perish. Worry is faith in reverse. Not only because most of the things we are anxious over never come to pass, but also because, when we worry, the most obvious things to do in our situation are overlooked, we should relax our tension by trusting God and putting at the disposal of that trust a clear head.

13.

When our minds are sick with frustration and division;
When fear eats away the foundations of our peace—
Be present, O, Our Father, to heal, to bless
and make whole.
When our hearts are heavy with sorrow and misery;
When only heaviness is our daily portion—

Be present, O, Our Father, to heal, to bless
and relieve.
When our friends are difficult because of misunderstanding
and loss;
When the beauty of comradeship has wasted like the noon
day—
Be present, O, Our Father, to restore, to
bless and renew.
When the thread of our years unwinds near the end of the
spool;
When the failing powers of mind and body accent the passing
days—
Be Present, O, Our Father, to reassure, to make
steady and confirm.
When our well ordered plans fall apart in our hands;
When hopes give up, having run their course—
Be present, O, Our Father, to replenish, to
create and redeem.
When faith in our fellows wallows in the mud;
When through disappointment, through failure, through
flattery, all seems lost—
Be present, O, Our Father, to revise, to renew and
reassure.

14.

THERE is much that has been written and even more that
has been said about "the will to live," in life in general, in

human life in particular. It is described as a quality inherent in life, an instinct with uncanny power to seek that which feeds and sustains it, however precariously. It is a wide and deep urgency with what seems to be a consciousness all its own. You have seen trees growing out of sheer rock; or roots, finding no soil below or being unable to penetrate the rocky substance of the earth, spread themselves, fan shape, on the surface, sending their tendrils into every crevice and cranny where hidden moisture and soil fragments accumulate. You have seen human beings with their bodies reduced to mere skeletons and all the vestiges of health wiped out—yet for interminable periods they continue breathing, as if to breathe were life. Sometimes this will to live takes other forms. Suddenly faced with some terrible moment of devastation, all the lights of the mind are turned out—one blacks-out. It is like coasting a car; the motor is turned off but it continues to move because of a cumulative momentum. Sometimes we escape into pain when not to escape seems to us to spell destruction. Again, the will operates in reverse: we escape into health. There is a real illness with which we cannot cope without disintegration, and we take refuge in the pose of health which, viewed from within, is not a fiction but a fact of experience. In the history of the religious experience of the race, doctrines of immortality are expressions of this will to live. They are not counsels of despair but deep affirmations of the core of life, declaring that life is continuous, permanent, timeless, eternal. What a tremendous boon, what a glorious outreach of the human spirit! The will to live says that life *is,* and it is not predicated upon any other factors. While life cannot be thought of as pure existence, yet it seems always to be *more than* that through which it expresses itself. Thank God for the will to live; it is His signature in the midst of the changing scene of experience and fact.

15.

A contemporary poet has written:

> Each night my bonny, sturdy lad
> Persists in adding to his, Now I lay me
> Down to sleep, the earnest, wistful plea:
> "God make me big."
> And I, his mother, with a greater need,
> Do echo in an humbled, contrite heart,
> "God make me big."

The simple desire of the average child is to become a big boy or girl. Time seems to stand still or to move backwards. Particularly is that true in families where there are several children or even two children of different ages. Sometimes the older child has more privileges, more freedom of movement, is treated in an adult manner by parents. All of this inspires in the younger the burning desire to move into a higher age bracket in order that the joys of riper years may be his. This is a most natural development and as such does not call for any special comment. But what the poet has in mind is something much more deeply interfused in the quest of the human spirit for a quality of life that is equal to the vicissitudes of experience. Many instances come to mind. Some person takes advantage of you in a situation and you are powerless to protect yourself or your interest. Days pass. Then, one day, the tables are turned and your most urgent impulse is to even the score. Much rationalization takes place. "I knew my turn would come," you say to yourself; "now I'll show him how it feels. Turn about is fair play, anyway. Besides, it is a bad idea for people to feel that they can do what he did to me and get away with it."—"God make me big," you whisper, as you turn aside from the temptation for revenge. Or it may be that you have impressed people with your ability or your genuineness of interest in an enterprise. You are faced with the opportunity to do a really significant job involving heavy responsibility. You cower in the presence of it. "I can't do that. I am not equal to it." Or, "I really am not interested in it to that extent." But there it is, and you have no available alternative but to tackle it. "God make me big," you cry out with all the power of your spirit. And then a strange thing happens. Strength comes from somewhere. The job does not seem as hard as it did before you tackled it. Deep within the task, something is released that eases the load; and the quality of your performance pervades your spirit with the assurance that God has answered. SO!

16.

It was just an ordinary dog in distress. My friend had never seen him before. Twenty minutes previously he did not know that the animal existed. Suddenly, he saw him struggling in shallow water, his body covered with a thick coat of crude oil. My friend stopped his car, jumped out, called to the dog but soon discovered that he was too exhausted to make the shore. Without a moment's hesitation, he went down into the water above his knees and so to the rescue. At first, the dog tried to get away, thinking that here was another enemy, or the same one who had thrown him in. At last, it was clear to the frightened animal that here was salvation. A complete change came over his entire body he relaxed, even as an automatic shiver passed over him, again and again. Together, dog and man, wet, oily and somewhat bedraggled, made their way to the nearest veterinarian. Arrangements were completed for the dog to be washed, treated and fed. Very often, we are reminded of the story of the Good Samaritan. We apply it almost instantly to stark human need when we are brought face to face with it. To apply it to so-called dumb animals requires an extra something, an added ingredient of sensitiveness. To meet human need, after all, may be regarded as an act of self-defense or the working out from under a bad conscience. To meet the need of an animal for which one has not developed any affection, is a mark of graciousness of spirit devoutly to be wished. As I reflect upon the meaning of this simple act as a revelation of the authentic character of my friend, I am moved to voice a simple thanksgiving to God that I know such a man. Are you such a person? Am I?

17.

The most difficult thing about learning to ride a bicycle is to keep one's eyes away from the obstacles, such as stones or bits of wood, that may be directly in one's path. The inclination almost always is to fix one's attention on the object so as to be sure to guide around it. Alas, the error! The surest way to guarantee that one will run over the object is to keep one's eyes focused on it. There is a sound principle here: an idea held steadily on a point of focus in the mind tends to express itself in action. This accounts, in part at least, for the fact that a person who has been cruelly treated over a long time interval tends to treat others in the same way when the tables are turned. It is not simply the desire for revenge or to take it out on someone else. The explanation is more deeply found in the fact that the sufferer has held his mind at dead center on the cruelty which he received until his own action pattern became integrated around cruelty. Left to himself, he behaves in accordance with the pattern that he has held steadily before his mind. This is not to argue that we should ignore the stone in the road or the cruelty to which one is subjected. But it is to remind us that we concentrate on either at our peril. Wise words—Where your treasure is, there is your heart also. Obviously, if we are to escape becoming evil in our behavior, we must bring our minds to bear upon the good and hold them there on dead center until our lives are organized on that basis. We are living organisms; we are not things. We become like the things we love. How wonderful, because it places so large a share of our destiny in our own hands.

18.

THERE is a fallow time for the spirit when the soil is barren because of sheer exhaustion. It may come unannounced like an overnight visitor "passing through." It may be sudden as a sharp turn-in on an unfamiliar road. It may come at the end of a long, long period of strenuous effort in handling some slippery in-and-out temptation that fails to follow a pattern. It may result from the plateau of tragedy that quietly wore away the growing edge of alertness until nothing was left but the exhausted roots of aliveness. The general climate of social unrest, of national and international turmoil, the falling of kingdoms, the constant, muted suffering of hungry men and starving women and children on the other sides of the oceans, all these things may so paralyze normal responses to life that a blight settles over the spirit leaving all the fields of interest withered and parched. It is quite possible that spreading oneself so thin with too much going "to and fro" has yielded a fever of activity that saps all energy, even from one's surplus store, and we must stop for the quiet replenishing of an empty cupboard. Perhaps too much anxiety, a too-hard trying, a searching strain to do by oneself what can never be done that way, has made one's spirit seem like a water tap whose washer is worn out from too much pressure. But withal there may be the simplest possible explanation: the rhythmic ebb and flow of one's powers, simply this and nothing more. Whatever may be the reasons, one has to deal with the fact. Face it! Then resolutely dig out dead roots, clear the ground, but don't forget to make a humus pit against the time when some young or feeble plants will need stimulation from past flowerings in your garden. Work out new designs by dreaming daring dreams and great and creative planning. The time is not wasted. The time of fallowness is a time of rest and restoration, of filling up and replenishing. It is the moment when the meaning of all things can be searched out, tracked down and made to yield the secret of living. Thank God for the fallow time!

19.

IT was a beautiful little garden just outside the dining room window. With the simplicity characteristic of him, my friend gave me the names and explained the habits of life of various plants growing there. I was struck by what was said about a little bush which grew near the steps. "This plant is called daphne. It is not doing well here because it is too comfortably situated. The soil is too rich, and it gets too much protection. This plant tends to go to wood and leaves with very, very poor blossoms if it is placed where it does not have to struggle. The aim of all plants is to reproduce themselves by making seeds. Poor soil challenges this particular plant, making it conserve its strength and concentrate it on the main business, the production of blossoms which in turn become seeds: the guarantee of the perpetuation of its kind." Then the silence fell while my mind took wings. An easy life devoid of challenge (too much protection) scatters the energy, dissipates the resources, works against singleness of mind, without which there can be no real fulfillment. Most of us do not voluntarily seek the difficult thing, the hard job, and the stubborn task. There are some people who are born with such singleness of mind that instinctively they gravitate toward the tough assignment. There are always those to whom we turn automatically if there is something to be done that requires unusual courage, patience or concentrated effort. These persons, by their temperaments and will-to-do, contribute deeply to our own delinquency and weakness. There are others who are afflicted with a morbid sense of martyrdom and who seem perpetually to be atoning for some hidden sin by volunteering to do the unpleasant thing, by taking upon themselves responsibilities which in the end merely deepen their own sense of guilt or self-mortification. It is wisdom so to understand oneself that one will not accept the role within one's range of choices that causes one to "go to wood and leaves." We are not like the daphne plant. Sometimes within very wide limits, often within extremely narrow limits, we have the privilege of choice. Some things we know contribute to our weaknesses, to our tendency to grow flabby and soft; some things we know toughen our fiber and cause us to pool all our resources in the effort to achieve singleness of mind, of purpose and of will. Wood and leaves, or the blossom of fulfillment—which?

20.

THERE must be always remaining in every man's life some place for the singing of angels, some place for that which in itself is breathlessly beautiful and, by an inherent prerogative, throws all the rest of life into a new and creative relatedness, something that gathers up in itself all the freshets of experience from drab and commonplace areas of living and glows in one bright white light of penetrating beauty and meaning—then passes. The commonplace is shot through with new glory; old burdens become lighter; deep and ancient wounds lose much of their old, old hurting. A crown is placed over our heads that for the rest of our lives we are trying to grow tall enough to wear. Despite all the crassness of life, despite all the hardness of life, despite all the harsh discords of life, life is saved by the singing of angels.

21.

OSCAR Wilde says in *De Profundis,* "There is always room in an ignorant man's mind for a great idea." It is profoundly significant to me that the Gospel story in Luke reveals that the announcement of the birth of Jesus came first to simple shepherds, who were about their appointed tasks. After theology has done its work, after the reflective judgment of men from the heights or lonely retreats of privilege and security has wrought its most perfect pattern, the birth of Jesus remains the symbol of the dignity and inherent worthfulness of the common man. Stripped bare of art forms and liturgy, the literal substance of the story remains: Jesus Chirst was born in a stable! He was born of humble parentage in surroundings that are the common lot of those who earn their living by the sweat of their brow. Nothing can rob the common man of this heritage. When he beholds Jesus, he sees in Him the possibilities of life for even the humblest and a dramatic revelation of the meaning of God.

22.

IT is a truth recognized over and over again in various guises that the key to the meaning of life is found deep within each one of us. When Jesus insists that the Kingdom of God is within, he is affirming that which is a part of the common experience of the race. Incidentally, this is one of the unique things about Jesus: he calls attention again and again to that which is so utterly a part of the deep commonplace experience of life. There is a story told of the musk deer of North India. In the springtime, the roe is haunted by the odor of musk. He runs wildly over hill and ravine with his nostrils dilating and his little body throbbing with desire, sure that around the next clump of trees or bush he will find musk, the object of his quest. Then at last he falls, exhausted, with his little head resting on his tiny hoofs, only to discover that the odor of musk is in his own hide. The key to the meaning of life is within you. If you have a glass of water out of the ocean, all the water in the ocean is not in your glass, but all the water in your glass is ocean water. This is a characteristic of life. The responsibility for living with meaning and dignity can never be finally taken away from the individual. Of course, there is the fact of limitations of heredity and the like, which may circum-

scribe decidedly the area of awareness within the individual
life; there is the total sphere of accidents which may alter the
mind and the spirit by some deadly seizure. But the fact remains that the judgment which the individual passes upon life
and by which life weighs him in the balance, finds its key
within the individual and not outside of him. It is the great
and crowning dignity of human life. Man rates the risk that
life takes by resting its case within his own spirit. How good
God is to trust the Kingdom of Values to the discernment of
the mind and spirit of man!

23.

To be alive is to participate responsibly in the experiences of
life. Men say grace at meat not only because they feel a sense
of gratitude to God for sustaining providence, but out of a
deep sense of responsibility to the life that has been yielded
in order that they may be sustained for one more day. The
bacon that a man ate for breakfast, at some moment in the
past, was alive with vibrant, elemental health and vigor. Who
can measure the reaches of aliveness of a hog, wallowing in
murky contentment in the summer sun? To what subtle overtones of aliveness is he responding in the guttural overflow
from his drooling mouth? There comes a day when he must
die—"be slaughtered" is the acrid word we use. What are
the paroxysms of lightning intimations of meanings that thud
through his body at the first fall of the bludgeon? In utter
accuracy, he dies that we may live. Thus, as we partake of his

body, we pause, like the stillness of absolute motion, to salute his leave-taking of life. Because of what he yielded and because of the myriad yieldings of many forms of life, we are able to live and carry on. This means that our life is not our own. Every minute of life, we are faced with the relentless urgency to make good in our own lives for the lives that are lost for us. Quite consciously, then, I see my responsibility to all that has gone into the making of me—not only in terms of food but also in terms of the total contribution that has been made to my life both by the past and the present. I must live my life responsibly or lose my right to self-respect and to integrity. This basic fact has profound bearing on the notion of freedom. Freedom means the possession of a sense of alternatives. It does not mean the absence of responsibility, but it does mean a sense of alternatives with reference to the experiences of life. If it be true, as we have pointd out, that to be alive is to be under active obligation to many other units of life, then the measure of my freedom is the measure of my responsibility. If I can do as I please without any sense of responsibility, then my alternatives are zero. I *must* select, *must* choose the option which will make possible the largest fulfillment of my own life plus the other lives of which I am the shared expression. One option is always available to me—I can choose the things for which I shall stand and work and live, and the things *against* which I shall stand and work and live. To yield this right, is to fail utterly my own self and all others upon whom I must depend. The highest role of freedom is the choice of the kind of option that will make of my life not only a benediction breathing peace but also a vital force of redemption to all I touch. This would mean, therefore, that wherever I am, *there* the very Kingdom of God is at hand.

Our Father, may our lives fulfill in themselves the hopes and unfulfilled yearnings of all whose stirrings for wholeness and completion are dim and inarticulate because of the burden of hate, weariness and misery under which their days are cast. May we achieve the freedom of sons of God, for whom every day is a Day of Judgment and every act a sacrament of thy Presence and every purpose a fresh channel through which thy Love pours forth its healing to the children of men. Amen.

24.

ONE of the great gifts of God to man is the sense of concern that one individual may develop for another, the impulse toward self-giving that finds its ultimate fulfillment in laying down one's life for his friend. It is difficult to keep the sense of concern free from those subtle desires to place another under obligation, and thereby stifle and strangle that which one wishes to bless and heal. When I ask myself why I try to help others, what reply do I get? Is it merely an effort on my part to build up my own sense of significance? Am I trying to prove my own superiority? When I do something for another which involves a clear definitive act of concern on my part, do I spoil it by saying to myself or to another, "Look what I did for him. And now he treats me as he does"? Or do we say, "After all I have done for him, he should do anything I ask of him"? Is our sense of concern used as a means for gaining power over others? To be able to give oneself without expecting to be paid back, to love disinterestedly but with warmth and understanding, is to be spiritually mature and godlike and to lay hold on the most precious possessions vouchsafed to the human race.

25.

EVERY person stands in need of forgiveness. No one escapes, however blameless his life may seem to him to be. This fact must never be forgotten. Let us examine the mechanism of forgiveness, perhaps for our own profit. In the first place I see the injury that I have done another as an *injury* and acknowledge it. But I must call it by its real name. If I have slandered, I must call it slander; if I have accused falsely, I must call it false accusation. Again, I must strip myself of all alibis and excuses. It may be true that I did not intend to do it, that it was all a hideous mistake; nevertheless, the injury may be as real to the other person as if my act were deliberately planned. Whatever may be the intent, the harm has been done. Again, I must seek reconciliation on the basis of my sense of responsibility, to the other person and to myself, for the injury done. Human relationships are often tough but sometimes very fragile. Sometimes, when they are ruptured, it requires amazing skill and sensitiveness to reknit them. Therefore, forgiveness is possible between two persons only when the offender is able to stand *inside* of the harm he has done and look out at himself as if he were the other person. One must remember also that guilt, however devastating it may be, is shared in some sense by the person who is injured. Why this is true, I am not sure that I understand, but that it is true, I have no doubt. There is scarcely a greater test of character than forgiveness.

26.

THE need for right desire is ever present. The Apostle Paul assumes right desire when he says, "I want to do what is right, but wrong is all that I can manage." It is in order, however, to raise the question of right desire because again and again we find ourselves doing precisely only what we desire to do. Sometimes we fail to be better than we are because we do not want to be better than we are. Have you ever said, "I know I ought to want to do this or that but the truth is, I do not want to do it"? With reference to our attitude toward other people, we say sometimes, "I know I should not feel as I do toward the Germans or the Japanese or the Negroes, but the truth is, I feel that way and I really do not want to feel differently. I know that I ought to want to, but I don't." The crux of the problem is not merely that we desire the right and find it difficult to achieve it, but it is also true that, again and again, we do not desire *to desire* the right. Few questions are more searching than "Do I desire to desire the right? Do I want to do other than I am doing? Do I treat people any better than I really want to treat them?" Utter candor demands that we face questions such as these. If we find the tragedy of our lives to be that we actually do what we want to do, then, at all costs to our pride, our fears, our self-righteousness, we must change our desiring. "Teach me to desire *to desire* the right, that I may be one with Thy Will and Thy Purpose."

27.

It is exceedingly difficult to keep from encouraging in oneself that which one condemns in other people. Vices are apt to take on the halo of virtues when they are part of one's own behavior, but seen in others they are regarded as being what in truth they are. If my neighbor squeezes the maximum amount of work out of a person for an absolute minimum of pay, I may certainly call it exploitation. If I do the same thing, I am apt to congratulate myself. What I would consider as a pose or pretense in my neighbor is apt to be called genuine when I do it. This tendency toward self-deception appears in one's attitude toward matters of social change. We tend to condemn in the system what we do not recognize in ourselves. Sins do not exist in general; they are specific, concrete, carrying their weight measured in terms of fearful accuracy. We do not sin against humanity; we sin against persons who have names, who are actual, breathing, human beings. The root of what I condemn in society is found at long last in the soil of my own backyard. What I seek to eradicate in society that it may become whole and clean and righteous, I must first attack in my own heart and life. There is no substitute for this.

28.

In Jesus' memorable conversation with Peter concerning the feeding of the sheep, there are two different words used for *love*. When Jesus says, "Simon Peter, lovest thou me?" Peter replies, "Yea, Master, thou knowest that I love thee." Jesus says, "Feed my sheep." The word Jesus uses for love is strong, dynamic, carrying with it the idea of reverential understanding and intelligent commitment. The word Peter uses in reply is weak, carrying with it the notion more of feeling than of understanding. It is the word which, in English, is most usually defined as love. Such words as philanthropy, etc., stem from this root. Three times Jesus asked Peter if he loved him. Three times Peter replied. But the third time there is a difference. Jesus uses the weak word for love and Peter is grieved, not because he asked him three times if he loved him, but because the third time Jesus, as an accommodation, shifted the demand from something that was at the moment out of reach to something that was more easily possible. The text would indicate that Peter felt that as long as he was faced resolutely with an impossible demand, Jesus was paying him the greatest possible compliment by thinking that he, Peter, could rise to such staggering heights. As long as this possibility remained before him, there was a chance for limitless development in that direction. When the ground was shifted to a less demand and the insistence to exert the last full ounce of spiritual energy was relaxed, Peter felt that his chances for stretching himself to the limit were short-circuited. Perhaps it is true that a goal that is in reach is not worth achieving. We find our true stature when we see ourselves in relation to a goal that can never be reached, to an end that can never be satisfied.

29.

DETACHMENT is often a method by which we can withdraw with some measure of poise and dignity from unpleasant things, even as we may be forced to maintain a routine relationship to them. The mind is doing this all the time. It makes a careful distinction between one's surroundings and one's environment. The environment is the result of selections from one's surroundings. It may be regarded as those aspects of one's surroundings to which one attends or which cause the reaction of attendance. A mother may sleep quite soundly through a thunder storm, but she will awaken instantly when her little child whimpers in the next room. This ability makes for a measure of sanity in modern life. Again, one may exercise detachment with reference to one's job. Even, sometimes, one attends religious services in that mood. Detachment becomes often a method by which we shirk responsibility and challenge. In the presence of human need, we may detach ourselves, on the ground that it is no concern of ours or that we do not wish to become involved or that we are too sensitive to expose ourselves to much that is distasteful. Charles Morgan in his *Flashing Stream* shows how this principle of detachment may operate in the life of a man who goes through a war as an officer while at the same time he does not permit himself to be involved in the sordid business. It must never be forgotten that we cannot escape a certain basic attachment in terms of responsibility for our world and the things that are done in it. This is an intimate part of the price we pay for being alive. Social responsibility does not provide for complete detachment, despite the fact that the point of direct participation in social sin may be several steps removed from my point of operation.

30.

THERE is often what seems to be a pardonable pride in achievement. But upon closer scrutiny, even this form of pride tends to make for arrogance. For it says that the achievement succeeded in capturing the thing envisioned. This is most often a mark of low aim. Any goal that can actually be achieved is perhaps not worth achieving; any dream that can be fully realized is perhaps not even worth dreaming. It is for this reason that we should have only pity and compassion for the great, for the man of apparently matchless achievements; the dream that he had was so much greater than the thing he has been able to achieve. When the man of real achievement compares the thing that he saw, that he used as a model, with what he has actually been able to do, he is filled with deep humility. What we see is what he has been able to achieve; what we do not see is what he saw in his vision. One day I remarked to a friend, "It must be a source of great satisfaction to you that you have been able to do so much for your daughters; by your hard work you are giving them the benefit of the best musical training obtainable in this part of the country." Her reply was simple: "Oh no, my one concern is that I am able to do so little of what I see that could be done." A man becomes proud and arrogant in his achievement only when he compares his achievement with other men's achievements, but when a man compares his achievements with his dreams, he feels ashamed that he has been able to catch so little of what he saw. Humility is the only mood that becomes him, and the only attitude. Approval in the last analysis can come from God and God only, because He alone understands the height and depth of an absolute demand.

31.

PRIDE and arrogance are always with us seeking to exert their pernicious influence in what we say and how we say it, in what we do and how we do it. No one of us escapes. Often we find ourselves most completely influenced by pride when surest that we are most self-effacing and humble. For the subtlest pose is that of humility and apparent willingness to be considered the least of all. Pride causes one to exaggerate his significance or insignificance, either by claiming for himself more than he knows to be true or by claiming for himself less than he knows to be true. It makes for fundamental dishonesty because it is just as false to underestimate oneself quite consciously as it is to overestimate oneself. Again, pride makes it difficult to see one's faults. For the badge of pride is self-righteousness. The mood that makes a person sure that he is always right, that his judgment is always sound, that he never stands in genuine error—it is often this that eats like cancer on the soul and character of the man on righteousness bent.

32.

God, I need Thee.
> When morning crowds the night away
> And tasks of waking seize my mind;
> I need Thy poise.

God, I need Thee.
> When love is hard to see
> Amid the ugliness and slime,
> I need Thy eyes.

God, I need Thee.
> When clashes come with those
> Who walk the way with me,
> I need thy smile.

God, I need Thee.
> When the path to take before me lies,
> I see it . . . courage flees—
> I need Thy faith.

God, I need Thee.
> When the day's work is done,

Tired, discouraged, wasted,
I need Thy rest.

33.

THE need for understanding grows out of the basic fact of
the unity of life. It takes many forms at various stages of
human development and experience. Sometimes, it expresses
itself in the play of little children, the girl fondling her doll,
the boy garnering his miscellaneous collection of pets, the
neighborhood gangs, and so on. For what is the meaning of
the devious ways by which we seek to identify ourselves with
other people, with other things, but a profound urgency for
self-revelation? It is the act of self-revelation that we anticipate
when we desire finally to be understood. The consciousness of
being understood by someone lifts to the level of awareness
the basic fact of unity that sustains and guarantees all of life.
We see the meaning of this clearly revealed in experiences of
loneliness. Loneliness is to be distinguished from solitariness.
In solitariness, a person is often most profoundly aware of the
underlying unity of life for it carries with it, often, a dimension
of sensitiveness to life, and awareness of others well nigh
unique. But the matter of loneliness is a different story. Loneliness means that the individual feels he is in isolation from
his fellows, cut off, stranded! The experience usually takes the
form of not being understood. When the Book says, "If God is
for us, who can be against us?" it is an insistence that, if the
individual has the profound consciousness that God under-

stands him, then this is the ultimate sense of unity beside which all the understanding of others, however reassuring, may seem of little consequence. The possible peril is that of self-deception. There cannot be any substitute for simple sincerity and searching honesty.

34.

Mood at High-Noon

Today is mine!
 You cannot take it from me.
 You can make it cloudy by your frown;
 You can fill me with sorrow by your tears;
 You can stifle me with torrents of despair.

But—

Today is mine!
 I can be quiet and hear what the silence brings;
 I can share freely my unstudied smile;
 I can feel kinship with the needy and the underprivi-
  leged;
 I can be indifferent and defiant, a lone tree in a forest.
 I can hate.
 I can love.
 What I do—matters forever!
 Today is mine.
  You cannot take it from me.

35.

A night so wild with the
        glory of the moon
        that the earth covered its face
        with
Silence.
On the pathway of my mind
        long, long thoughts run riot.
They are quieted; not by the
        beauty of the moon
On the covered face of the earth—
But by the passionate swelling
        of awful harmony:
"De Ole Sheep, they know the road.
Young lambs must find the way."
My heart whispers to God:
"Let me always be the young lamb."

36.

THE cult of inequality appeals to all of us in some of its
aspects. One of the most subtle forms of its appeal is in the way
in which it inspires us to think that life will always make exceptions in our case. We think that the things that apply to
the rest of mankind do not apply to us. We are exceptions be-

cause we belong to the cult of inequality. This often has a special appeal to youth. Because I am young, I say to myself, "The things that *I* do, do not count. Life will make an exception in my case because I am young." Most persons who are in positions of power belong to this cult. Again and again, power causes us to feel that we are outside of the operation of the normal moral or physical laws. What applies to the persons of less power than we have does not apply to us. We are exceptions. Many Christians belong to this cult. Because they are Christians, some people are convinced not only that they are better than "the lesser breed without the law," but also that they have an inside track with God. The Cult of inequality is the breeder of one of life's greater illusions; namely, that exceptions will be made in our case because we *belong*.

Our Father, teach us that "nothing walks with aimless feet" and that the history of our life is its own judgment.

37.

THE central emphasis of the teaching of Jesus centers upon the relationship of individual to individual, and of all individuals to God. So profound has been the conviction of Christians as to the ultimate significance of his teaching about love that they have rested their case, both for the validity and the supremacy of the Christian religion, at this point. When someone asked Jesus what is the meaning of all the law and the prophets, he gave those tremendous words of Judaism, "Hear, O Israel, the Lord thy God is One, and thou shalt love the Lord thy God with all thy mind, heart, soul and strength. Thou shalt love thy neighbor as thyself." Jesus rests his case for the ultimate significance of life on the love ethic. Love is the intelligent, kindly but stern expression of kinship of one individual for another, having as its purpose the maintenance and furtherance of life at its highest level. Self-love is the kind of activity having as its purpose the maintenance and furtherance of one's own life at its highest level. All love grows basically out of a qualitative self-regard and is in essence the exercise of that which is spiritual. If we accept the basic proposition that all life is one, arising out of a common center—God, all expressions of love are acts of God. Hate, then, becomes a form of annihilation of self and others; in short—suicide.

38.

I$_T$ is exceedingly difficult to live one's life creatively and effectively without developing what may be called a sense of fancy. An important distinction must be made between a sense of fancy and a sense of fact. A sense of fancy seems to be the particular gift of little children. They people the world with living fairies and elves; the little girl carries on a real conversation with her doll; Santa Claus does come down the chimney, and he has reindeer and a sleigh, and he does live at the North Pole, spending all the time between Christmases making toys for little girls and boys. Of course, if this sort of thing persists into manhood and womanhood, the individual may be regarded as being somewhat off-balance. But what is basically present in a sense of fancy must continue to influence the attitude and outlook of the individual toward the world and toward people. This unique element has to do with imagination, with the ability to envision things in terms of their highest meaning and fulfillment, even as one grapples with them in the present as they are. It is not to disregard the sordid, the mean, the thing of low estate in one's life, or one's experiences with others, but it is to deal with these aspects of life in the light of their highest possibility. The sense of fancy then broods over the meanness of man until there begins to appear in one's relationship with him, growing edges that are full of promise—that are not mean. I repeat, it is not to ignore the fact that the man is mean or devilish or prejudiced, but it is to recognize that this in itself is not a complete picture of the man. There is something more there. A developed sense of fancy illumines the dark reaches of the other person until there is brought to light that which makes for wholeness and beauty in him. This is what God is doing in human life all the time.

39.

. . .There's magic all around us
In rocks and trees, and in the minds of men,
Deep hidden springs of magic.
    He who strikes
    the rock aright, may find them where he will.[2]

[2]"Watchers of the Sky" from *Collected Poems in One Volume* by Alfred Noyes. Copyright, 1922, 1950, by J. B. Lippincott Co. Reprinted by permission.

It is very easy to assume an attitude of indifference toward the ordinary commonplace aspects of life. This is natural because constant exposure to experiences tends to deaden one's sensitiveness to their meaning. Life does grow dingy on one's sleeve unless there is a constant awareness of the growing edge of one's experience. The mood of arrogance toward the ordinary person and the tendency to grovel in the presence of the high and powerful beset us all. This is due to the deep quest of the human spirit for status, for position, for security-rating. I remember once meeting a most extraordinary man on a certain college campus where I was giving a series of lectures in religion. Each morning he sat in the front seat. He was a cripple— he walked suspended between two huge crutches. At the close of the last lecture, he came up to me. "Mr. Thurman, you have been very kind to me during this week. I want to give you something. Will you come to my room this evening when you are through with your work?" It was agreed. In the interval I asked one of the students about him. I was told that he was an old fellow who earned his living by repairing shoes in a shop on top of the hill. Some of the students referred to him simply as "Old Crip." When I entered his room in the late evening, he was standing behind a chair supporting himself very deftly. "Mr. Thurman, do you like Shakespeare? What is your favorite play?" "*Macbeth*," I replied; then, without further ado, he read for me from memory the entire first act of *Macbeth*. And at my dictation, for over an hour, he read scene after scene from Shakespearean tragedies. He was just an old crippled man earning his living by repairing shoes for college men who thought nothing of him. There is magic all round us. It may be that the person with whom you live every day or with whom you work has, locked deep within, the answer to your own greatest need if you know how to "strike the rock aright."

40.

THE ability to bring all the impulses and desires of one's life under the control and domination of a single dedication is of the greatest significance for the religious man. Such ability is the secret of power in all undertakings and is the basis of true spiritual growth. There can be no meditation until the mind and spirit have been brought to a point of focus upon some central notion or idea, and held there until the extraneous elements are sloughed off and there is well nigh complete absorption. Have you ever tried to pray, but your mind kept wandering? And then at some other time you were able to bring all of yourself to bear upon a central concern before you, resulting in a fresh lift of spirit and a new sense of calm. The same necessity for focus is present in the matter of the development of character. I was walking with a friend one day along the shore of the Jumna River in Allahabad, when we noticed not very far ahead a small group of people standing around a man who was speaking. We approached close enough to hear what he was saying. He was a strange-looking man—a holy man, his body, covered with holy ash, completely naked except for a loin cloth. Squatting at his feet was a lion. For a moment I was most uncomfortable. I asked my friend to interpret what he was saying. This was his message: "Behold this lion. I found him in the foothills and taught him how to bring under subjection all of the wild and unrestrained animal impulses of his nature so that now he is gentle and harmless. Go then and do likewise with the stubborn and unyielding impulses of your own nature." He moved on and repeated it at another spot before a group that had gathered. Hard of accomplishment as it is to bring one's appetites and desires under subjection to a single holy purpose, it is even more difficult to *fashion* such a purpose. One reason why high dedication is so difficult is to be found in the fact that it is extremely arduous to formulate for oneself a purpose that is sufficiently high to be challenging and, at the same time, capable of demanding the consent of both one's mind and heart. To so much, one's heart may say, "Yes," while the mind says, "No." War at one's center—this is the tragedy of modern man.

41.

In the presence of human need, the Christian is faced with the subtle temptation to substitute indignation for some practical step of ministry. Sometimes the sheer horror of human suffering is so seering that the immediate reaction is one of shock. How often do we hear words like these: "How terrible! My, how awful! What a tragedy! Have you heard of anything so shocking!" All of this is perfectly natural in the presence of the overwhelming and tragic. But we must be careful not to let all our energy escape in outcries and indignation so that there is nothing left but exhaustion. One's emotions may be so explosive that they quite take the place of some more sig-

nificant form of help or alleviation. The outburst is confused
with other forms of action and one becomes quiescent when
in reality nothing has been done. Often this takes the form of
righteous indignation. It is to be remembered that there can be
no righteous indignation that is not penitent. When righteous
indignation has a core of penitence at its center, then it leads
to some form of responsibility usually expressing itself in
action. Another temptation in the presence of human need is
quite consciously to reduce one's exposure to pain by keeping
oneself from direct contact with it. The principle of alternation
is most important here. Obviously, one cannot maintain a continuous contact with human suffering without making some
kind of radical emotional adjustment to it. Therefore, one
should alternate one's contacts. Carry the burden, actually, and
then put it down. Carry one's vicarious load by seeking to redeem and to heal, and then let it go. If one does this, then it
is easier to seek and to find the key to that which is big enough
to absolve one from artificial and ineffective attempts to meet
human need.

42.

HE is just a lawyer with a breezy, "free wheeling" manner.
Why he studied law remains his secret. His interest is not primarily in making money, but he manages to carry his end of
the stick without too much difficulty. Watching him function
in a committee meeting, or heeding the salty quality of his
speech, one would not think of him as being religious in the
conventional sense. On first encounter, one is struck by his

apparent lack of inhibitions. His mind is like well-honed steel, vibrant, sharp and strong. His face is that of a man who has seen much, understood even more, and remains completely unafraid. There is no piety here. One hardly imagines seeing him kneel before an altar (though he does), because he prays best on the wing. The most deeply moving characteristic which he possesses is an authentic interest in people who are being harassed by life, and the discriminating use to which he puts his intelligent and informed good will. He is never too busy to counsel those who find their way to him, even though what they are able to give in terms of dollars is negligible or even nonexistent. When he is faced with a complicated social problem concerning which the law is at variance with his high sense of decency and human dignity, an exhilaration is apparent in the quickened tempo of speech and the telltale flash of the eyes. Life seems to him to be a fascinating and ever-eventful adventure. When he has been most helpful by putting at one's disposal the results of his legal training and his fruitful years, he gives the impression that to be of service is a privilege and a joy. To him, the legal profession is a vehicle through which he gives expression to his profound commitment to the purposes of God among the children of men. To be tender without being soft, to be gracious without being officious, to be kind without being condescending—this is the fine art of living which he manifests with increasing contagion. It is always reassuring to encounter such a man, because it keeps alive one's personal confidence in one's own essential worth. To call such a man a friend raises a joyful shout in the heart.

43.

WHETHER your childhood was sad or happy as you look
back upon it, there is one thing about it that is true. There
were moments of intense and complete joy, which for the
instant left nothing to be desired. It may have been your first
new dress, or new suit; the thing about which you had dreamed
for, oh, so many days was actually yours! Perhaps it was the
first time you received a letter through the mail; your name
was actually written on the envelope and it had come through
the mail; yes, the postman actually brought it. It may have
been your first time to visit a circus to see live tigers, lions,
elephants and big, big snakes; and there was the merry-go-
round and the fluffy candy and the cold pink lemonade. Perhaps it was the time when your mother let you mix the dough
for the bread or sent you on your first errand in the next block
alone. You may have been eavesdropping when the teacher
came to call and you heard her say how smart you were and
what a joy you were to teach. (And you wondered whether your
mother would remember to tell your daddy what the teacher
had said. At supper you managed to bring it up, so that your
mother would be reminded.) Your greatest moment of fullness
may have come when, for the first time, you were conscious
that your mother loved you—that swirling sense of sheer
ecstasy when you were completely aware of another's love. Do
you remember? It was a foretaste of something for which you
would be in quest all the rest of your days: the matured relationships of friends and loved ones, of husband and wife; and
that gradual or climactic moment of religious fulfillment when

the heart and mind echo the words of Augustine: "Thou hast made us for Thyself and our souls are restless till they find their rest in Thee!"

44.

AGAIN and again, we are impressed with the fact that little things can make big differences. A little act of kindness at a moment of great need makes all the difference between sunshine and shadows. A smile at the right moment may make an intolerable burden lighter. Just a note bearing a message of simple interest or concern or affection may give to another the radically needed assurance. A simple "Thank you" has softened many a hard situation or punctured the crust of many a "hardboiled" person. There is always a place for the graceful gesture, the thoughtful remark, the sensitive response. It is what may be called "living flexibly." There is often confusion between formality and ungraciousness, or informality and graciousness One may be gracious without fawning and affectation. There is no greater compliment to be given than to say: "You are very kind. To know you is to make life itself a more satisfying experience." This means that such a person has learned, or developed, or been born with, the fine art of gracious living. It is the antidote to much of the crudeness and coarseness of modern life. Our reputation for bad manners and for rudeness is unenviable. The derogatory names that we use to tag other peoples and other races, the supercilious flippancy used as the common coin of daily intercourse, all these thing reflect a carelessness in living that hurts and bruises, often where there is no intent to injure and destroy. It is true that little things often make big differences.

45.

I<small>T</small> is easy enough to be gracious and sympathetic with other people when they are in dire need or facing some great tragedy. Most people rise to meet a crisis in themselves or others. It is a far greater test of character to be kind and gracious, when there is no special need, when the situation is not heightened by any unusual demand. It is not difficult to believe in America when the national life is threatened by some foreign enemy who would overrun our shores and establish a form of government that stands in radical contrast with our own. It is a far greater test of political faith to believe in America when there is no great external threat knocking at our door, only the corroding work of domestic unrest and betrayal. It is often a simple matter for men to have an outburst of faith in God when the ground is cut away from beneath their feet by sudden death or overwhelming disaster. Even the most secular-minded person may find himself saying, at such a time, "Good God" or "God have mercy." But it is a far greater test of what a man lives by when, in the midst of the monotony of the daily round, he keeps alive a sense of wonder, awe and glory. A contemporary poet, after outlining the irreverence of modern man— "The moon is cold, a vulcanized crust, no shine, no spell, no glory; God is a myth, a Sunday story"—says: "And yet, they cry to God when their children die."

46.

OLIVE Schreiner attaches a significant footnote to her discussion on "Parasitism" in her volume entitled, *Women and Labor*. It is the story of an old mother duck, who brought her latest brood of ducklings down beside what had been a pond. Since her previous ducklings were born, the pond had become baked mud. The duck urged her little brood to go in and swim around, to eat worms and chickweed, where no water, no worms, and no chickweed were; while they with their fresh young instincts smelled the chickweed and heard the water 'way up the dam. They left their mother beside her old pond to go in quest of water and of food, perhaps to get lost on the way or perhaps to find it. To their old mother they said, "Can't you see that the world has changed? You can't bring the water back into the dried-up pond. It may have been better and pleasanter when it was there, but now it is gone forever. Would you and yours swim again, it must be in other waters." There is an element of grave risk in all adventure. On the cover of a pacifist magazine published in England before the last war, there appeared this striking sentence: "It is madness to sail a sea that has never been charted before; to look for a land, the existence of which is in question; if Columbus had reflected thus, he would never have weighed anchor, but with this madness he discovered a New World." The reassurance of a secure income, the quiet glow of working with a safe and respected institution in conventional ways, the sense of well-being that comes from being accepted by everyone because one's thinking is "sensible" and safe, all of this makes for a certain kind of deep tranquility. But there is apt to be no growing edge and very little of the tang and zest of aliveness that only the adventurous spirit knows. It is not an accident that the messengers of the gods were symbolized as human beings with wings, ages before men thought of the possibility of flying through the air. The God of life is an adventurer and those who would affirm their fraternity must follow in His train.

47.

"WHEN two individuals," writes Dr. William A. White, "be they cells or organisms, unite for a common purpose—let them be two men, A and B, who come together in a partnership for carrying on some sort of business—the union of A and B in such a partnership is not expressible by adding A and B together and setting down the results accordingly. There is something else that has gone into the formula besides A and B, a third component, and that third component is the relationship between them." The instant we read the quotation, we recognize it as a statement of fact we have known all along. There are various names by which this third component is called: understanding, awareness, appreciation, sympathy, kinship, friendship, and even love. It is compounded of a thousand little overtones revealed by a crucial smile, a characteristic gesture expressing worlds of unspoken meaning, an unconscious comment, more of reflex than reflection, and a direct question asked with no answer expected. Once a joint quest is undertaken, there is an irrevocable commitment to a deepening of the understanding of each other on the part of those who share in the enterprise. "The third component," "the bond between," is often an unconscious knitting of organism to organism, of life to life. It is the quiet extension of the self to include more and more of another. This bond between can never be directly sought; it appears as a by-product of association, of working together. The demands that it makes are never direct and formal, they are often subtle and compelling. There is something profoundly reassuring about the experience itself, for it means that, at last, there is someone who understands some full measure of my life, and, in that understanding, I may find strength and confidence for my life's adventure. There are deep perils here, for the "bond between" can be turned to ill account through weakness, blindness or crass egotism. To regard the third component as a creative moment when the finite mind is illumined by a vast infinitude is to recognize that truly in His own image did God create the men of earth.

48.

THE Apostle Paul writes to his young friend, Timothy, saying, "Do thy diligence to make thy voyage before winter." I would like to add a line to the injunction, taken from a speech I heard many years ago: "There is a time of snow in all adventure." If the two sentences are connected by the simple word "because," a suggestive idea is revealed. The revised passage would read, "Do thy diligence to make thy voyage before winter because there is a time of snow in all adventure." The temptation to put off the important decision, the crucial conversation, the beginning of the exacting task, and the living of life seriously is ever present. When we are young, it is easy to say that we cannot begin to take our responsibilities until we are older. The fatal words are, "There is always time." What has happened about that important book you were going to read? What about that friend who misunderstood you? Weeks and months ago you were planning to sit down and talk it through, but you have not done it. There is that letter you were going to write when first you heard that an acquaintance of other years had fallen on evil times, but it has been a year and a half now, and it seems too late to write the letter. The time of snow has set in. Sometimes, in private conversation or in a meeting, an opportunity appears to say the right word, to save a situation, or to bring about a new and creative attitude toward an old problem, or to protect a defenseless absent person; and we let the opportunity pass by default. After that, we may discover that there is little if anything that can be done. There is a time of snow in all adventure, and we forget it to our peril. This injunction is radically important in preparation for tasks to be done. When our preparation is superficial or careless, the real significance shows up when we go into production, and then it is apt to be too late—the season of snow is upon us. How long must have been the preparation before a beautiful thing like a rose could appear! What travail must be borne before the earth is peopled with whole, integrated persons!

49.

THERE is always something impressive about a fresh start. Think how fortunate it would be if time was not somehow divided into parts. Suppose there were no day, only night. Even in parts of the world near the North Pole, there is a six month day and a six month night. Or suppose there were only winter, or only summer, or only spring. Suppose there were no artificial things like months so that we could not be mindful of the passing of time. Suppose there were no years, just the passing of hours with no signposts to mark them into units of months and years. Then there would be no New Year. The beginning of another year means the end of a year that has fulfilled itself and passed on. It means that some things are finished, rounded out, completed forever. It means that for some of us certain changes have taken place that are so profound in their nature that we can never be what we were before. There is something so final, so absolute, about a year that is gone. Something of it remains in us that we take into the year that is next in line. But the New Year means a fresh start, a second wind, another chance, a kind of reprieve, a divine act of grace bestowed upon the children of men. It is important to remember that; whatever the fact may have been, it cannot be undone. It is a fact. If we have made serious blunders, they are made. All our tears cannot unmake them. We may learn from them and carry our hard-won lessons into the New Year. We can remember them, not with pain, but with gratitude that in our new wisdom we can live into the present year with deeper undertanding and greater humanity. May whatever suffering we brought on ourselves or others, teach us to understand life more completely and, in our understanding, love it more wisely, thus fulfilling God's faith in us by permitting us to begin this New Year.

50.

AGE is a matter of perspective, attitude and digestion. There are many people who are young in years but are old in reactions, who have lost their resiliency and are already exhausted. There are others who are full of years, chronologically, but who continue to be alert, sensitive and elastic. For most people, it is difficult to accept the fact of increasing years. The human body tends to prepare the mind for old age by providing the basis for a kind of covering philosophy. When a sixty-year-old person sees someone half his age leaping up the stairs four at a time, he says to himself, "How stupid to wear yourself out in needless exertion!" All of us must accommodate ourselves to the simple fact that we are not so young as we once were, and thus take life in the stride belonging to the years we have lived. A friend of mine gave me, the other day, a copy of a prayer written by a lady past ninety years of age. Her whole life had been spent in Elyria, Ohio. This is her prayer:

O God, our Heavenly Father, whose gift is length of days, help us to make the noblest use of mind and body in our advancing years. According to our strength, apportion Thou our work. As Thou has pardoned our transgressions, sift the ingatherings of our memory, that evil may grow dim and good may shine forth clearly. We bless Thee for Thy gifts and especially for Thy presence and the love of friends in heaven and on earth. Grant us new ties of friendship, new opportunities of service, joy in the growth and happiness of children, sympathy with those who bear the burdens of the world, clear thought, and quiet faith. Teach us to bear infirmities with cheerful patience. Keep us from narrow pride in outgrown ways, blind eyes that will not see the good of change, impatient judgments of the methods and experiments of others. Let Thy peace rule our spirits through all the trials of our waning powers. Take from us all fear of death, and all despair, and undue love of life; that, with glad hearts at rest in Thee, we may await Thy will concerning us, through Jesus Christ our Lord. Amen

51.

ANY serious thought concerning death must somehow deal with the fact that death is not the worst thing in the world. The dramatic fact about death is its apparent finality. Because we seem paralyzed in the presence of so tremendous a fact as the complete cessation of all human activity on the part of a loved one, the reaction of dread and panic in some form seems natural. And yet, a moment's reflection makes us aware that there are things in life that are far worse than death. Every person can make his own list and for some people, I suppose, there would be no list. Men in all ages and all periods of human life have found this to be true. Such an idea indicates a gross conception of the immortality of man, gross because it is inexhaustive in its desperation. It is the ultimate guarantee, the sense of alternative in human life upon which, in the last analysis, all notions of freedom finally rest. Here is a recognition of death as the one valid option which can never be taken from man by any power however great, or by any circumstance however fateful. If death were not implicit in the fact of life, then in no true sense would there be any authentic options in human experience. This concept regards death merely as private option for the individual: *private* because it involves the simple individual as if he and he alone existed in all the world; *option* because, while it assumes the inevitability of death as a factor, it recognizes the element of timing, which brings this inevitable factor under some measure of control. In other words, even though it be true that I *must* die, it is also true that I can exercise some control over *when* I die. Death, therefore, is a part of experience, it is an event in life. It not only affects man, but man in some sense knows that he is being affected by it. A man is a spectator, an observer of his own death. It is something that is happening to him. To the degree that it is possible for me to know that I am not exhausted by death, something remains, something that is untouched, even by so crucial an experience.

52.

IT is a great temptation to try to escape responsibility not only for one's own actions but also for one's own privileges. Responsibility means, essentially, standing up to be counted. It means the ability to look things squarely in the face and pay the price for what one does. In a family of children, there are usually at least two types represented. There is the child who always says, "I didn't do it," or "Betty made me do it, so it is not really my fault," or "I wasn't thinking when I did it. I am sorry." Such expressions become a substitute for facing the consequences of one's deeds. It is an easy settlement of one's personal account by deferring to someone else. Such children usually grow up to become adults who increase the tasks and the work of all with whom they come into contact. When they marry, the wife or husband is always to blame for whatever happens. The net result is a quality of self-righteousness, a "King-can-do-no-wrong" aroma, which makes life difficult for those who must bear the burden of enduring it. The other type of child is one who is ever eager to take on more than his responsibility, particularly more of the blame, than he should. This means two things: (1) Other children easily learn to exploit and abuse him, because their weakness is aided and contributed to by the willing burden-bearer. (2) The sense of being a martyr becomes acute. This is self-righteousness in reverse. Of course there is a place in the world of weakness and temptation to come to the rescue, to take on responsibilities equal to one's strength, to make life a bit easier for the overtaxed and depressed. Such zeal must not perpetuate weakness and turn into permanent cripples those who might find their own feet and strength by being compelled to stand up in their own right and be counted for what they *do*.

53.

ONE of the most striking paradoxes in life is this: as children we spend much simple anxiety in an effort to act like grownups; when we are adults we seek to recapture some of the simple things that were ours as children. To be an adult means, of course, to be mature, somewhat hard or rigid, to say the least. For many, it means to be sophisticated and to lack sentimentality. For still others, it means to be cynical and untrusting. It may be instructive to examine a few of the characteristics of childhood that would greatly improve life, if they were developed through the years of chronological maturity rather than cut off. I name first, a simple honesty. A child *is* what a child *does*. Whereas, to be adult means to become increasingly skillful in "throwing the stone and hiding the hand." This virtue in children, simple honesty, becomes sincerity when it matures. All great religions, whatever may be the radical differences in their interpretations of the meaning of life, of God, or of man, are agreed in their insistence upon an almighty sincerity. In recent years much of the healing work of medicine and psychology has had to do with the function of genuineness as a therapeutic factor in human life. Another manifestation of simple honesty on the adult level is dependability. There are few reassurances comparable to that which is present when one knows that he is dealing with a person who is dependable, whose word counts in terms of specific values. Another characteristic of childhood is the sense of wonder, of awe, of mystery. It is the reverse of the bleary-eyed picture of many adults who have lost the sense of wonder in living. They have tasted all experience, they have no response for surprises, for that which is breathlessly beautiful. They are world-weary, incapable of the tremor of sheer delight or the thrill of intense awe and wonder. Essentially, they are emotionally frayed, played out, or encrusted. There is much in modern life that makes for that end result. To recapture the wonder of little children, to know once again the fresh feel of the unknown as we stand on the threshold of new adventure, this saves life from boredom and keeps it from growing dingy on our sleeve.

54.

WHAT a priceless gift is memory! Suppose you had no memory, how difficult life would be; every day, and every minute in the day, you would have to begin everything for the first time. Learning would be impossible and education would be meaningless. We have the amazing power to carry along with us, moment by moment, a vast accumulation of things done, of experiences lived through, of skills and techniques that have long since been learned by heart and put aside to be brought promptly into play on demand. It is in order to raise the question as to the use that is made of memory. How

do you use it? There are some people who use their memory
to store away all the unpleasant things they experience. Every
slight they have received from the hands of another is neatly
labeled with the offender's name and put away as in a card
catalogue. When some later contact with the person is made,
they run through their files, lift out the old offense, and dress
it up to be paraded in the new encounter. The habit grows,
until at last their storehouse is full of unpleasant things which
send their poisonous fumes all through the corridors of the
mind, filling them with suspicion, resentment and hate. There
are others who use their memories to store away the pleasant
things of experience. Such memories become a vast storehouse
to which, at a minute's notice, they turn to restore their faith
and re-establish their confidence in life, at difficult and trying
times. The next time you feel that life is mean or completely
evil and that there is no good in it for you or anyone else, try
this: make a list of some of the beautiful things you have seen,
the breathlessly kind things people have done for you without
obligation, the gracious moments that have turned up in the
week's encounters. Memory is one of God's great gifts to the
human spirit without which neither life nor experience could
have any meaning. Moreover, without it we could not be
human beings.

55.

I T is a matter of amazing significance that the Creator of life
assumes that human beings are able to absorb most of the

negative and destructive things that happen to them without disintegration and collapse. There is nothing more staggering to contemplate than the sheer endurance of personality. It is tender and tough. It is soft and hard. It is lucid and opaque. Even the human body exhibits staggering endurance. In a book like Cannon's *The Wisdom of the Body,* the significance of such a remark becomes clear. Almost all "well" people are fighting and winning in their bodies the battle of disease. Or consider the adjustment that one has to make to noise. Have you ever picked out the different noises heard on a busy city street? Every single sound takes its minor or major toll of energy from one's storehouse, and yet these sounds can be so absorbed that the emotional balance of the personality will not be thrown off. Such an item alone is crucial. Or think of what is required in making one's adjustment to all sorts of people with whom one is thrown into more or less direct contact. The people with whom one works and who may be mutually irritating, or the people with whom one lives, may require major adjustments in order to keep the emotional balance. Some years ago, a farmer gave two apples to a friend of mine, visiting in the State of Washington. Each apple had a deep scar extended from the stem half way around the circumference. The scar was marked by shriveled apple flesh. The rest of the apple had grown rounded-out, but the dead place remained. The story the farmer told my friend was this: When the apples were very young on the trees, a hail storm bruised them deeply. The apples did not rot, they did not fall off the tree; they did live. It was as if they decided to absorb as much as possible of the violence of the hail storm and go on with the business of self-realization. The world is full of people who are like the apples. It is the greatest tribute to personality that the Creator of life assumes that each manifestation of life will have enough inner strength to fight its battles with such simple tools as may be at its disposal. A part of the business of living is to get better tools and to increase the tool-technique, but the fundamental assumption remains.

56.

THERE is something incomplete about coming to the end of anything. This is true even though it may be the close of something for the end of which we have longed for many days, or even years. There is the end of a long siege of illness, when the surge of new strength and vigor pervades one's entire body and the mind begins to pick up a fresh attack upon the world of men and things. The days in bed, the routine of the sick room, the frequent and periodic visits of the doctor, the solicitation of friends and loved ones, the silent watches, the night with the voices that can be heard only when "day is done"; all these have become a part of life's pattern. But this is over. There is the end of a voyage after days on board ship. The endless promenading on the deck, the long, lazy afternoons, the unique smell of the cabin, the new friends, the storms, the circuitous fascination of the sea, all this is behind at voyage-end. There is the end of friendship. The early days when affection was tender and the ιours of anxiety during new unfoldings were safely passed; the period when tokens of testing were everywhere; the moments of mounting ecstasy when the sheer joy of aliveness overflowed, feeding all the valleys of the soul; the long days of tranquility when nothing happened because one had seeped quietly through all open things; then the end—no sharp break, no vast upheaval, only the quiet closing, one by one, of doors. There is something incomplete about coming to the end of anything. Even the end of life does not seem final, notwithstanding one's attitude toward life after death. The fact is, one never comes to the end of anything. Something always remains, some deposit, some residue that mingles with the stream of one's life forever. In a sense, there can never be an end of anything; something remains. This is what is meant by the words Tennyson placed on the lips of Ulysses: "I am a part of all that I have met." True also is it that all I have met is a part of me, forever.

57.

ARE you a member of Self-Righteousness Anonymous? It is an organization without structure, without form, without location, and without offices. Every person who belongs to it holds all the offices at one and the same time, for each member is the organization. It is a very old group, as old as the first mistake. Its watchword is bigotry. Of course it does not mean to be intolerant, bigoted and "upright." But that is the way it happens. Its numbers are always right. In every discussion their word must be taken at its face value. Others may have to prove what they say, make a clear case for their position;

not so with S. R. Anonymous. When he speaks, Truth has spoken. When he is tolerant, it is a benevolent toleration, the kind that a German police dog may have for a poodle pup. Of course such a person does not make mistakes. To be sure, mistakes occur in his career, but they are always due to extenuating circumstances for which someone else is responsible. Such a person cannot be challenged. When you challenge him, you are being unreasonable, or self-willed, or stubborn. There is a smugness about him that inspires ill-will. Jesus describes such a man who went up into the temple to pray. He said to God, "Lord, I thank thee that I am not as other men. I pay my vows. I offer my prayers. I am a good man. I pause in the midst of my well-organized righteous life to let Thee know how good I am." The picture is overdrawn. It is almost a caricature. Nevertheless, the sober truth is clear. All of us are candidates for Self-Righteousness Anonymous. One of the sure results of self-examination in the light of the Highest is an immediate humility and a canceling of one's membership in Self-Righteousness Anonymous.

58.

THERE is something always challenging about an inaccessible mountain peak. Men spend months, often years, fitting and equipping themselves for the grand undertaking. The fact that such a peak has never been scaled before, that many others have tried, only to lose their lives in the quest, all adds to the zest and urgency of the tremendous effort. Men feel this way about trying to scale Mt. Everest, for instance, not merely because they may want fame or acclaim but because here at last is a challenging test of all their powers. In measuring themselves against the mountain, they get some fleeting glimpse of their own basic merit. In the realm of ideals and man's relation to them, we encounter the same mood. An ideal that men can master, can fulfill, is not worthy of them. It does not provide an authentic test. What men crave for is to be faced with some impossible demand, some challenge which leaves them exhausted in the fulfillment. In the last analysis, men have but contempt for that which is well within their powers of achievement. This is no test of their powers, even when it is completely achieved. A religion that places before men goals that can be reached, ends that can be completely satisfied, is a bad religion. The glory of religion, even as of life, is the fact that when men have utilized their powers to the full, there remain stretching out before them vast reaches of the yet unexplored. At their best, men are willing to settle for the highest; anything less than that at long last merely contributes to their delinquency and snatches from their hands the bracing vigor of infinite development and growth.

59.

SOME years ago, I read, in *The Christian Century,* a poem that described the fate of a young woman whose brightness had faded and whose brilliant thoughts had turned quietly to a whitened ash. The remark was made, in a comment about her, that she reminded one of a conversation between a man and his gardener. The gardener spoke about two young apple trees that had shriveled up one spring. "They died," he said, "of too much blossoming." The idea here is one that has profound meaning. One naturally thinks of youthful vigor and enthusiasm when the blood is warm and hopes are high, and the frosts of ripening years have not worked their work. The perennial energy of youth, expressing itself in a wide variety of ceaseless activity and apparent restlessness, is a constant source of renewal for those whose steps have slackened with the years. The caution of the poem is profoundly urgent. If all the strength of youth goes into blossoming, if there is no holding back, no restraint, nothing will be stored up against the time when a supreme effort is needed to do the long, drawn-out, difficult thing. Many older people exploit youth at this point. They fasten themselves, with weary tentacles, into the robustness and verve of youth, hoping that what is equivalent to a blood transfusion will take place in their own lives. It is a desperate reach for life. There is yet another dimension in which the idea has relevance. We are tempted to spread ourselves very thin by full-scale participation in every activity. It becomes a kind of disease which saps the strength so that one becomes increasingly incapable of real performance. Dr. Cabot of Harvard told me about an address he delivered before the National Conference of Social Workers on "The Limitation of Intake." He had stressed, for comparison, that the number ten bears the same relation to infinity that the number one million bears. If human need is infinite, one may work twenty-four hours a day for a thousand years, and at the end, human need will still be endless. A quantitative judgment cannot be made upon that which is qualitative. The wise person, then, relaxes on quantity and concentrates on quality. It is good to remember the poem about the

> Two young apple trees that shriveled up one spring;
> They died from too much blossoming.

60.

No life is complete that does not make provision for the place and significance of ceremonials. They are the moments of pause, of tarrying over meanings, of high celebration. There are those who regard all celebrations as sentimental, as a sign of immaturity and childishness. Nevertheless, we cannot escape the need for those experiences which summarize for us the inner meaning of the commonplace. For some of us, these experiences take the form of personal ritual growing out of a set way of doing things. It may be putting out one's own clothes for the next day, the final ceremonial before getting into bed. It may be taking a sip of coffee before tasting any other food at breakfast. It may be arranging one's shoes in a certain way. I know one person who, when he receives a letter from a special friend, carries the letter in his pocket unopened, reading it only at the very end of the day when he can give himself over completely to its overtones. There are certain ceremonies in families, celebrating birthdays in an especially private manner. I know one family that does not open Christmas cards until after breakfast on Christmas morning. Because religion has to do with the inner meaning of human experiences, a large place is given to ceremonials and to rituals. It is easy for ceremonials to disintegrate into props and stage setting. But this tendency should not cause us to underestimate their significance. One of the central ceremonials of the Christian religion has to do with the death of Jesus. It is called by various names, the Lord's Supper, the Last Supper, the Holy Communion, etc. It is meant to celebrate the meaning of the life and death of Jesus, the central figure of Christianity. It dramatizes the tragic sense of life and the meaning of suffering as an expression of the redemptive power of God in human life. It calls attention to the moral power of fellowship among men, even as it recognizes the essential loneliness of all human life. All men who have tested their own integrity against devastating pressures, who have been true to their convictions even though the battle was lost, who have turned a soft answer without fear under the withering assault, know the inner meaning of the high moment in this Christian ceremonial. They know this and share its secretive power, whether they bow their knees before any altar or confess any name. In the last analysis, if a ceremonial is authentic, its inner meaning is universal.

61.

I was standing on the corner waiting for a streetcar, when I noticed a man seated behind the steering wheel of an automobile parked on the opposite side of the street. He was busily engaged in making notes in a little book. Presently he put his book away, started the motor, and then looked over in my direction with a broad, inviting smile on his face. I smiled in return, thinking at once that in some way our paths had crossed. He opened the door of the car, called to me, extending an invitation to ride downtown if I were going in that direction. As we rode along, I listened for some word in the conversation that would reveal his identity or the fact that, at some time in the past, we had met. It was soon clear that we were total strangers, but that, out of the graciousness of his heart, he had offered me a lift. He was just a salesman, speaking with a broken accent, who was glad of the chance to share what he had with someone whose need was specific at the point of his fullness. I was reminded of a very precious friend who has the habit of stopping at a certain corner each morning, offering a ride to any person who may be standing there waiting for the car to go uptown. According to the testimony of this friend, each morning was a heightened adventure in understanding a new person, a different person. A rare richness has accrued to her because of the cross fertilization of so many different human beings with whom she has shared a practical fullness at the point of a practical and felt, immediate need. Perhaps there is nothing more exhilarating to the spirit than to be able to minister to the needs of others at the time when a particular need is most acutely felt. This is the essence of the spirit of Christmas. We spend much time and energy during this season of the year in selecting gifts to be given to our friends. Very often these gifts are shared with the desire that they will make the right kind of impression on the receiver; sometimes the impression that we seek to make is in terms of our abundance, or our discriminating taste, or our hope for something of like kind in return. Very rarely indeed is our giving out of the fullness of our possessions at the point of our friend's greatest felt need. The result is that Christmas means fatigue, exhaustion, a kind of world weariness, that makes for self-pity. It must be borne in mind that true friends are those who accept us as we are, for what we are in ourselves. Their affection and their understanding cannot be purchased by gifts. A thoughtful telephone call on Christmas Eve or Christmas Day, a hand-written note of intimate recollections, will often lift up and strengthen the heart of another, leaving a long, sustaining afterglow when a gift, however costly, will only be a gift. The true meaning of Christmas is expressed in the sharing of one's graces in a world in which it is so easy to become calloused, insensitive and hard. Once this spirit becomes a part of man's life, every day is Christmas, and every night is freighted with anticipations of the dawning of fresh, and perhaps holy, adventure.

62.

OUR life represents essential process. It is small wonder that classic Buddhism makes so much of the experience of flux in human life. We seem always to be on our way. When I was ten years old, I said that the thing I sought would come to pass when I was fifteen. When I became fifteen, it would come to pass when I was eighteen. On and on through the years, it is around the next turning. Life is like that. Growth is made possible in human life because of this essential characteristic.

I shall arrive! What time, what circuit first
I ask not; but unless God sends His hail,
Or blinding fireballs, sleet, or stifling snow,
In some time, His good time, I shall arrive!
He guides me and the bird. In His good time.

We are never able to do anything in quite the way we want to
do it. No single experience, however great, is quite able to
represent us adequately. Life is essentially dynamic and alive.
It is this particular manifestation of life, by which we are surrounded and of which we are a part. With reference to no experience are we able to write Q. E. D. Life is essentially unfinished. All judgments concerning experience are limited and
partial. It is for this reason that, in the last analysis, judgment
belongs with God. Even our self-judgments are limited because we can never quite get out hands on all the materials, all
the facts in each case. In any total sense, we must act on the
basis of evidence that is never quite conclusive.

63.

THE disintegration of human life is always difficult to handle
emotionally. The wasting away in illness, the gradual fading
of one's intellectual powers, the quiet ebbing of physical
energy, all these are a part of the disintegration of human life,
with which we have to do. One watches the appearance of the
first strand of gray in the hair and then, quickly or creepily,
the hair blossoms with heavy frost; or the first signs of bald-
ness, and then more and more, until one's face extends up be-

yond the horizon to find fulfillment in a hairy fringe on the back of the head just above the neckline; or the first crow's feet around the eyes, and then here and there a wrinkle, and then more and more, until at last the fact of ripeness of years or premature physical cracking must be dealt with fully. At such times we are apt to feel as if life is taking unfair advantage of us, stripping us of all defenses of self-respect against the world. As we watch our own powers fade, or those of our friends, we wish that life were not so tenacious. Why cannot we make a clean break of life without wasting away? It is humiliating. When such thoughts crowd into one's mind, it is good to remember that it is precisely the tenacity of life, the way in which life squeezes each solitary bit of energy out of every available source, that has made survival possible and the endurance of the "slings of outrageous fortune" within the range of the creative powers of the human spirit. Man is tough! Man's body is tough! Man's mind is tough! Again and again, the story is that man crumbles rather than crashes. (For the first time in our history, the tempo of life is so heightened that there may not be time enough to crumble, only to crash.) Life is alive and every tiny rootlet and every tiny nerve cell charged with the energy of the eternal. Old age, sickness, the fading of the powers is fought inch by inch all the way to the grave. Hallelujah!

III

A Sense of Presence

FINALLY, there must be a matured and maturing sense of Presence. This sense of Presence must be a reality at the personal level as well as on the social, naturalistic and cosmic levels. To state it in the simplest language of religion, modern man must know that he is a child of God and that the God of life in all its parts and the God of the human heart are one and the same. Such an assurance will vitalize the sense of self, and highlight the sense of history, with the warmth of a great confidence. Thus, we shall look out upon life with quiet eyes and work on our tasks with the conviction and detachment of Eternity.

1.

WHENEVER the mind of man has been uplifted; whenever I have frustrated the temptation to deny the truth within me, or to betray a value which to me is significant; whenever I have found the despair of my own heart and life groundless; whenever my resolutions to be a better man have stiffened in a real resistance against some form of disintegration; whenever I have been able to bring my life under some high and holy purpose that gives to it a greater wholeness and a greater unity; whenever I have stood in the presence of innocence, purity, love and beauty and found my own mind chastened and my whole self somehow challenged and cleansed; whenever for one swirling moment I have glimpsed the distinction between good and evil courses of conduct, caught sight of something better as I turned to embrace something worse; whenever these experiences or others like them have been mine, I have seen God, and felt His presence winging near.

2.

NOT only is faith a way of knowing, a form of knowledge, but it is also one of life's great teachers. At no point is this fact more clearly demonstrated than in an individual's growing knowledge of God. It is obvious that, in the last analysis, proof of the existence of God is quite impossible. A simple reason for this is the fact that, if there is that to which God may be finally reduced, then He is not ultimate. But let us not be led astray by this apparent abstraction. Faith teaches a man that God is. The human spirit has two fundamental demands that must be met relative to God. First, He must be vast, limitless, transcendent, all-comprehensive, so that there is no thing that is outside the wide reaches of His apprehension. The stars in the universe, the great galaxies of spatial groupings moving in endless rhythmic patterns in the trackless skies, as well as the tiny blade of grass by the roadside, are all within His grasp. The second demand is that He be personal and intimate. A man must have a sense of being cared for, of not being alone and stranded in the universe. All of us want the assurance of not being deserted *by* life nor deserted *in* life. Faith teaches us that God is—that He is the fact of life from which all other things take their meaning and reality. When Jesus prayed, he was conscious that, in his prayer, he met the Presence, and this consciousness was far more important and significant than the answering of his prayer. It is for this reason primarily that God was for Jesus the answer to all the issues and the problems of life. When I, with all my mind and heart, truly seek God and give myself in prayer, I, too, meet His Presence, and then I know for myself that Jesus was right.

3.

THE second thing that man's faith teaches him about God is that God is near. One of the *Sayings* of Jesus discovered among the papyri at Oxyrhynchus is this: "Jesus saith: 'Wheresoever they may be, they are not without God; and where there is one alone, even then I am with him. Raise the stone, and there thou shalt find Me; cleave the wood, and I am there.' " Isaiah gives a vivid picture of Jehovah, a vision which came to him during the year of the death of King Uzziah. He saw the Lord on a great white throne, high and lifted up, and His Glory filled all the temple. Jesus erected a pyramid out of the funded insights of all the prophets, scaled its heights and brought God down out of the clouds, and found Him to be an intimate part of the warp and woof of human experience and human struggle. Very often, we find it difficult to think of God as a part of life because we associate Him rather exclusively with the supernatural, the miraculous, the unusual. He belongs in the *special services* division of human life, where only the rare and extraordinary aspects of life are to be found. It was this conception that Jesus sought to undermine in his day. If God be far away, then He comes to us only on rare occasions and in rare situations. Of course, there is a sense in which this is true; the high moment, the great experience, the supreme challenge, the poignant sense of great contrition, all these may mark a sense of special Presence. But we do not live in such rarefied atmosphere. What we most want to know about God is whether He is present in the commonplace experiences of ordinary living, available to ordinary people under the most garden variety of circumstances. That God is not far from any one of us is the essence of the Gospel which Jesus proclaimed. "Closer is He than breathing, nearer than hands or feet."

4.

FINALLY, faith teaches us that God is love. This is a very difficult affirmation for the human spirit at times, because of the overwhelming amount of human misery and suffering by which our days are surrounded. All over the world, at this very moment, there is agony deeper than any formula of expression, the dumb inarticulate throb of which can only be sensed by a sympathy and understanding infinite in quality and limitless in grasp. Too, so much of human misery is poured out upon the innocent and helpless that life seems to be possessed of a vast, hideous deviltry. Of course, there has never been a completely satisfying answer to human suffering, particularly as to the *why* of it. It is clear that the profoundly significant reflection upon the misery of life must begin not with an idea of omnipotence but with the concept of love. But a step from the conception of God as the perfect Knower men come inescapably to the conception of God as perfect love. To know fully is to understand and to understand is to care. The reason for affirming that God is love is based upon the fact that, in human experience, men discover that love is the most inclusive and completely inexhaustible aspect of life. Again and again, men have found that they will do gladly, for someone for whom their love is vast, what no power in heaven or hell could make them do if they did not love. Where love is great, we do for the beloved things which would be completely revolting if love were not. At every level of human life around us, we see this in operation. Therefore, whatever else God is, He must be love. He must be one with the most completely all-embracing, all-inspiring experience of human life. It is for this reason that, when a man is sure of God, God becomes not only his answer to the deeper needs of life but also sustaining confidence as he moves out upon the highway of life to meet the needs of other men. Wherever such a person goes he *is* a benediction, breathing peace.

5.

PRAYER grows out of an imperative urgency, sometimes pointed, sometimes diffused. It enables one to keep fresh and focused in spirit the dedication to which one's life is given. Again and again, it creates a profound sense of power deep within the mind, expressing itself in strange new courage and purposefulness. The first manifestation of this courage is the attack that it makes on the basis of one's external fears of people and of circumstance. Prayer often yields a buoyancy and joyousness of spirit as the overtone of a relaxed confidence in God. It helps to clarify the conflicting issues that naturally arise out of any form of action, so that, against the darkness of the age, I can see the illumined finger of God guiding me in the way that I should go; so that, high above the clash of arms in the conflict for position, for rights, for status, for security, I can hear speaking, distinctly and clearly to my own spirit, the still, small voice of God. Without this, nothing quite has meaning; with this, all the rest of the journey, however difficult, however painful, however devastating, will be filled with a music all its own, and even the stars in their

courses and all the wooded world of nature will participate in
the triumphant music of my heart.

6.

All night I lay across my bed—
No rest—no sleep;
Nought but the utter agony
    of despair.
I cried to God—
The answer: Bald, awful silence.

Along the walk outside my
    window
A group of men—
Students in a Southern school—
    return
From breakfast.

Suddenly, as if in answer to my
    all night cry,
They wooed the silence into song:
    "I'm so glad trouble don't las' always,
O my Lord, O my Lord, what shall I do?"

7.

"Take time to be holy" is a familiar line in a hymn that was often sung in many churches a generation ago. The notion is that spiritual life requires cultivation, development, and is not a gift merely. For such a process, time is of the essence. Mark you, not time in terms of clock hours, necessarily. Not always time in the sense of duration. Time is of the essence in developing the inner life because, without a large sense of leisure, the external world with its demands, emergencies and crises, chokes the flowering of the mood of Presence. As a college student I was very much influenced by an associate who was the most active man in college—he was a debater, a star in the annual Shakespearean play, a member of the glee club, a flutist in the orchestra, an end on the football varsity for four years, a star guard in the basketball quintette, and withal, a major in chemistry and a man about town. The thing that was unique about Jack was the sense of leisure that he seemed to carry about him. He had a quality of unhurried ease that gave strength and dignity to his acts. It seems to me that spiritual maturity is to be thought of in terms of poise and roominess. It is easy to substitute fussiness and meticulous attention to all kinds of details, for strength either of mind or of character. There are some people whose very presence inspires a relaxation of inner tensions. To come in contact with them is to find one's confidence restored by a general atmosphere of spaciousness and tranquility. Such a quality may be a sheer gift of God, but, more often, it is the result of profound cultivation of those inner graces called into life by the quickening Presence of God, made manifest in a sense of leisure in the midst of the activities and pressures of daily living.

8.

Do I believe in God? Again and again, I ask myself the question. It is a searching query and one that cannot be answered by a "snap" reply, whether it be negative or positive. A belief is a thing upon which a man may stake his life and practice, to the extent that the object of one's belief has to do with that which is central to one's life. If my belief has to do with something that does not really matter, or matters little, then only a small part of my life and practice may be dependent upon it. But if my belief is relative to the most important thing in my life, then my belief becomes the mainspring of my life and practice. There are two important aspects to belief. There is a sense in which belief may be taken for granted as the basis for thought and action. It may not enter into my mind as a conscious influence but rather be the sure foundation upon which I build my attitudes, thoughts and behavior. In this sense, I may not be "belief-conscious" at any particular moment, but my belief may pervade my life like an aroma. The second aspect of belief has to do with the deliberate ordering of one's life, quite consciously, in accordance with the demands of one's belief. On this level, the content of my belief must be as intelligent as possible. I must know what it is that I believe and why. It is in this area that the question raised at the beginning of this meditation becomes profoundly relevant. If I believe in

God in this sense, precisely what do I mean? It would be helpful to our own spiritual growth and understanding if we put down in order on paper what we mean when we say we believe in God. Try it. Then put the paper aside, and in several months or weeks, make another list and note what has happened to you in the interval.

9.

It does not require the expert knowledge of the psychologist to discover that we live daily under conditions that undermine whatever tendencies there are in the human spirit that make for a relaxed way of life. Everyone is in a hurry. There is little time left for the deep experiencing of the facets of life that make up the daily round. In our homes, someone spends many hours in planning, shopping for and preparing food. Mealtime often is something to be rushed through in the shortest possible time. Thousands of years were spent in the developing of our taste bulbs. We scarcely use them now. What a joy it is to linger over the taste of food! In a simple thing like bread that is thoughtfully and carefully prepared, one may taste the richness of wheat or corn or barley that in its growth absorbed sunlight and rain and the rich chemistry of the soil. All the ingredients besides should serve to reveal and make available what the grain has stored up in its life under the skies. Or take the matter of conversation. Go back over the days of this very week. How much good talk have you had? What a history a word reveals of the strivings and the triumphs of the human spirit! Do we select our words with the kind of reverence that bespeaks a recognition of the treasure house they bear? The spoken word is the symbol of meanings that we try to convey by conversation. Our conversation is hurried, feverish, hectic. Our spirits do not have time to use our words as lungs through which they breathe. To have a good talk—to have times of sharing through the spoken word deep things of the mind— leisure to search for the right word that is capable of channeling the stirring of things within—this is to have the mood to linger in conversation. Or take the matter of a sense of direction for one's life. Do you take time to ask, "What is my point? What am I trying to do with my own life?" All travelers, somewhere along the way, find it necessary to check their course, to see how they are doing. We wait until we are sick, or shocked into stillness, before we do the commonplace thing of getting our bearings. And yet, we wonder why we are depressed, why we are unhappy, why we lose our friends, why we are ill-tempered. This condition we pass on to our children, our husbands, our wives, our associates, our friends. Cultivate the mood to linger. If you do not know how to start, or if the conditions under which you live make it difficult, try getting up earlier on Sunday morning and establishing a meditation period. Who knows? God may whisper to you in the quietness what He has been trying to say to you, oh, for so long a time.

10.

I⊤ is a simple story, simply told. One day, a man walked into an antique shop and asked permission to look around. It was a rather exclusive shop frequented only by those who could afford to purchase articles made rare by their scarcity and age. The visitor seemed strangely out of place because he was poorly dressed though clean; indeed it was clear from his appearance that he was a laborer whose face had been etched by sun and rain and whose hands were rough and worn. After more than a half hour, he left. In about ten days he returned. This time he found a very beautiful piece of old glass and asked if he could make a deposit on it. Each week he made a payment, until at last the article was his. With much curiosity, the owner of the shop engaged him in conversation to determine, if he could, the use to which such a man would put his new purchase. "I bought it for my little room. It isn't much, but I bring to it, from time to time, through the years, only the very best and most beautiful things. You see, that is where I *live*." To bring to the place where you live only the best and most beautiful—what a plan for one's life! This is well within the reach of everyone. Think of using one's memory in that way. As one lives from day to day, there are all sorts of experiences, good, bad, beautiful, ugly, that become a part of one's past. To develop the ability to screen one's memory so that only the excellent is retained for one's own room! All kinds of ideas pass through one's mind, about oneself, about the world, about people. Which do you keep for your own room? Think it over now; which ideas do you keep for the place where you live?

It is well within the mark to say that the oft-quoted words of Jesus, about laying up for yourself treasures in heaven, deal with this same basic idea. The place where you live is where your treasures are. Where your treasures are is where your heart is. Where your heart is, is where your God is.

11.

FRANCIS de Sales, in his *Introducion to the Devout Life,* says that bees, when they are surprised by the wind, lay hold of little stones so as to keep their balance and not be swept away by the storm. No one is able to predict when, and indeed how often, the strong winds will come to threaten the very core of one's balance and security. Indeed, there are some people whose lives seem to create vacuums that pull into them tempests, storms, tornadoes, which keep them constantly in a state of siege. For such, there does not ever seem to be the lull, the quiet period, when nothing is happening. It may be that such persons regard the quiet time merely as that which is the immediate forerunner of the storm and hence cannot be separated from the storm. Often, as a mere "technique of equilibrium," an attitude or mood is developed that makes the individual hold his course, despite the fact that his way ever moves along the storm paths. There may be an element of fun and good fortune in the fact. The rest of us, however, live very tame lives. We are not often caught up in blowings that would uproot and make havoc with our balance. But, soon or late, we are visited by the storms. Sometimes they come unannounced—bright sunshine one moment, and the next dark clouds and the winds. Sometimes they are a long time in the making. We may ignore the signs for we may be too busy to be able to do anything to prepare for meeting them. At any rate, there comes a day when all fury breaks forth and we are without shelter, without protection. At such a time, we are reminded by Francis, the bee fastens himself onto a stone which is nearly always at hand, and clings to this, thereby enabling him to keep his balance and not be swept away by the storm. Do you have anything to which you cling at such times, that enables you to keep your balance and not be swept away by the storm? Think it over.

12.

HE was a man of medium height, with a relaxed face and quiet eyes, dapper in appearance in a saintly manner. For more than twenty-five years he was a professor of New Testament at the Graduate School of Theology at Oberlin College. His name: Edward Increase Bosworth. I met him one day in the town haberdashery while he was in the act of selecting a necktie. The clerk informed me that it was a very painstaking task always when some article of wearing apparel was being chosen. I stopped by the counter for a word of greeting. "I am trying to select a necktie," said he. "I believe that a man is under moral obligation to give to people who look at him, as completely satisfying an experience as possible. The clothes a man wears are also a part of the sacrament of living." Another time, I was working in a student conference in Wisconsin,

when I had a long conversation on prayer with a man who had
spent some twenty years as a Y.M.C.A. secretary in China.
Without my knowing quite how it happened, the conversation
turned to Dr. Bosworth. My friend said, "When my daughter
was in her early teens, she was having a very tempestuous time
with her emotions. My wife and I were completely stumped.
We were living in China and felt helpless to do the thing
which she needed. As a matter of fact, we did not know what
she needed. Then I thought of Dr. Bosworth and decided to
write him a letter asking him if he would include our daughter
in his list of persons for whom he prayed each day. I received
an immediate reply in which Dr. Bosworth expressed his concern. He said that it was impossible for him to include our
daughter in his list, because his list was full. Then there followed a most amazing comment. As nearly as I can remember
it, it was this: 'I do not think that I should have more people
on my list than I can attend to thoughtfully and prayerfully
in the period of my day that is specifically set aside for that
purpose. A man must mean business with all of the powers of
his mind and spirit when he lifts another person in prayer to
God. When there is a vacancy on my list, I will include Mary.' "

13.

A few days after Dr. Bosworth's death, I went up on the
campus to visit the library in Council Hall, the theological
building in which Dr. Bosworth had had his office. I stopped
at the entrance to chat with the janitor. I remarked, "We shall

certainly miss Dr. Bosworth in the village." The janitor answered, "I don't think that anyone else will miss him in quite the way I shall miss him. During the many years that I have been here as a custodian, he was my friend. Many times in the winter, when I was shoveling snow, I have seen him walk across the campus, going two blocks out of his way just to tell me good morning. Every time he spoke to me, I felt that I was more of a man than I was before his greeting." The great Dr. Bosworth, honored on both sides of the Atlantic among countless students and others for his New Testament scholarship and the crystal saintliness of his beautiful life, walking two blocks out of the way to say good morning to the janitor! For many years, it was customary in the village for the churches and the college to unite in a Thanksgiving service in Old First Church. After the sermon, there was a period given over for testimonials, during which time individuals, as the spirit moved, would rise to give vocal expression to their thanksgiving to God. This particular morning, a very elderly Negro lady arose to speak. She had learned to read when she was sixty-two years old, in order that she might read the Bible for herself. She was overcome with emotion; at length she recovered her bearing and said simply, "I know that my redeemer lives, for he lives in my soul. Glory Hallelujah!" When she sat, there was a breathless silence. Into the stillness came the quiet voice of Dr. Bosworth, "What the sister has just said is the final word that the human spirit has to say about the meaning of life and the meaning of God. I rejoice to be in her fellowship, and I can only repeat her words, 'I know that my redeemer lives, for he lives in my soul. Glory Hallelujah!'"

14.

WHAT is the source of your joy? There are some who are dependent upon the mood of others for their happiness. They seem bound in mood one to another like Siamese twins. If the other person is happy, the happiness is immediately contagious. If the other person is sad, there is no insulation against his mood. There are some whose joy is dependent upon circumstances. When things do not go well, a deep gloom settles upon them, and all who touch their lives are caught in the fog of their despair. There are some whose joy is a matter of disposition and temperament. They cannot be sad because their glands will not let them. Their joy is not a matter for congratulations or praise; it is a gift of life, a talent, a gratuitous offering placed in their organism. There are some who must win their joy against high odds, squeeze it out of the arid ground of their living or wrest it from the stubborn sadness of circumstance. It is a determined joy, sharpened by the zest of triumph. There are still others who find their joy deep in the heart of their religious experience. It is not related to, dependent upon, or derived from, any circumstances or conditions in the midst of which they must live. It is a joy independent of all vicissitudes. There is a strange quality of awe in their joy, that is but a reflection of the deep calm water of the spirit out of which it comes. It is primarily a discovery of the soul, when God makes known His presence, where there are no words, no outward song, only the Divine Movement. This is the joy that the world cannot give. This is the joy that keeps watch against all the emissaries of sadness of mind and weariness of soul. This is the joy that comforts and is the companion, as we walk even through the valley of the shadow of death.

15.

It was the celebration of the Passover, the common meal of surging remembrance. The Master and his twelve disciples were gathered around the common board. Many and varied were the thoughts that streamed in endless procession through their minds. During the last few days, a strange and ominous quality had entered into the warm intimacy of the fellowship. The smell of death was in the air. There were many things that had been left unsaid through all the previous days, but now they clamored for utterance. But there were no words made ready. As it turned out, this was the last real calm before the precipitous days ahead, ending in the lacerating moment of the crucifixion. The last common meal. In the light of the events that followed it, every single detail of the meal was highlighted with a rare and awful radiance. Every accent in retrospect told its own sure tale. There was something living once, which, if it could be recaptured, would bring again into the midst the spirit of him whose magic had led captive their spirits, and once more they would know the comfort of his presence winging near. The experience is a part of the human story. Suppose you and a friend had dinner together one evening in your home. A few days after, the word came to you that the friend was dead. You would crawl inch by inch over all the events of your last meal together: The fact that you had inadvertently given to him the chipped cup. You did not discover it until, in the candlelight, the chipped spot was revealed as he lifted it to his lips to drink. Given the fact of his passing, you read back into all the common talk of the evening many things that were not present at the time, but now are clear. Gently you put away the chipped cup. It can no longer be the common thing it was before. Perhaps in certain rare moments, when you wish particularly to have the memory of your friend very living, very present, very real, the cup is used again. It is symbolic of a whole lifetime of knowledge and sharing, which you and your friend had known. The cup becomes the reminder that you have shared deeply the spirit of your friend, and that is yours forever. Death could not touch it—he could never die. And so it would be all the way to the end. The communion service, the celebration of the last supper, stripped bare of all that devotion has done in beautiful liturgy or somber dogma, means that, when spirit invades spirit, the eternal in one man mingles with the eternal in another, transcending time, space, and all the artificial barriers by which one man is marked off, separated from his fellows. To those who have learned the mind and the teaching, the courage and the wisdom of the simple Master of Galilee, the sharing together of the common meal in the holy place is to usher into their midst spirit of his spirit and mind of his mind. "Yes," he says to all, whatever may be their faith, creed, doctrine or persuasion, "when in your fellowship you eat your common meal, remember me."

16.

"My God! My God! Why hast Thou forsaken me!" According to the Gospel of Mark, these are the final words uttered by Jesus before his death. They reveal at once one of the most amazing utterances in the entire literature of religion. Here is one who was convinced that he had followed the will and the leadings of God through all the shifting scenes of his life at a most crucial moment in the development of his own people. He had experimented effectively and conclusively with love and understanding as a way of life; he had spent long hours in prayer and meditation; he had given himself with increasing intensity to a full-orbed understanding of the mind of God, whom he interpreted as Father. The logic of his life had led him to the fateful agony of the cross. He was there keeping his tryst with his Father—but where was his Father? The implication of the cry, which Jesus quotes from one of the Psalms, is that he was surer of God than God was of him. It means also that, in his moment of complete exhaustion, Jesus was making one of the great elemental discoveries about the nature of existence; namely, that often the point at which man becomes most keenly aware of the reality of God is on the lonely height, when he is stripped to the literal substance of himself, with nothing between his soul and an ultimate agony. At such a moment, God is seen as the only reality, and oneness with Him as the only fulfillment. The secondary meaning of this discovery is that the end of life and the meaning of life cannot be summarized in terms of happiness, joy, or even satisfaction. Again and again, we must discover that life may say "No" to our most cherished desires, our high hopes, our great yearning. And we must learn to live with life's "No." This is not only to discover the peace that passeth understanding, which may come when the pain of life is not relieved, but also to know for oneself that God is closest to us when, in our agony and frustration, he seems to be farthest away.

17.

Millions of men and women are unwilling to accept the fact of death as a final and exhaustive fact in human experience. This unwillingness expresses itself in various ways, sometimes by a quiet adjusting of one's personal timetable to the inevitable passing out of life as a definite human entity. The moment death is adjusted to, in this sense, it loses its threat and fades as a menace. Soon or late, all of us come to the realization that "one by one the duties end; one by one the lights go out." Sometimes we regard death as merely an episode, a chapter in a book, not the whole book. Man is a time-binder as well as a space-binder. Have you noticed how often you seem to be outside of the things that are happening to you, watching them as an observer? Whatever the experience may be, it is never quite exhaustive, there is always some corner of you that is the observer. We come to regard all experience as taking place within a certain compass, and, in a sense, we are outside looking on. Why should death be any different? It is quite unconvincing to say that death swallows life. The coming of spring is one of the happiest symbols in the experience of the race, a perennial reminder that death is but one aspect of experience, a phase of life in transition and a lag in the vast creative process of life itself. It is small wonder that, in the Christian tradition, spring and Easter merge into a glorious expression of the aliveness of life.

18.

ONE of the most positive expressions of the life of God in the life of man is the gift of imagination. If it were not for the imagination, reflective thinking would be quite impossible. Memory would be mere physical sensation that had left its traces in the nervous system. It is unlikely, even, that human speech would have developed at all. Think of it: because of the gift of imagination, you can go back into the past, relive experiences that are no longer present, leap into the future, anticipate that which is yet to come, walk through a wall, or span an ocean in the twinkling of an eye. Perhaps most important of all, without imagination human love would be impossible of achievement, for there can be no love among human beings where there is no power of self-projection. The mechanism of love is the ability to put oneself in the life of another and to look out upon the world through the other's eyes—to enter into the feeling and thinking and reacting of another, even as one remains oneself. This can never be done completely; hence the element of profound frustration and tragedy at the center of the love experience. Imagination is the creative vehicle that carries one spirit into the dwelling place of another. There could be no sympathy in the world if men had not the gift of imagination. The spirit of man could never take flight in dreams, hopes or aspirations if there were no wings of imagination given as a part of man's equipment for life. Man would merely be his little self—no more, no less. There could be no hope for anything beyond. Think of it, just to be myself, myself alone, knowing forever that nothing could ever happen to me that would go beyond my present self! But the witness of God's spirit in man's spirit is symbolized by imagination, without which there could be no sense of sin, no repentance and contrition, no tenderness and sympathy, no love and no hope.

19.

HE had buried sixty American sailors who had lost their lives in the fearful bombing his ship had been given in the early afternoon. As the chaplain and his group of men started toward the landing crafts, one of the sailors said, "Sir, there is another body over there, a Jap." The chaplain looked, while saying with just a slight tone of irritation in his spirit, "What, another one!" He was tired, nauseated, and exhausted in body and spirit. The men were all for throwing the dead man in the bush, as they had become accustomed to doing. The chaplain bent over to examine the body, to discover that he was the pilot whose ship had done so much damage to their outfit. It was a moment of great searching of hearts. His mind was made up. He called his men together and addressed them as follows: "Men, we must find the right thing to do this afternoon, the right thing to do in the light of Eternity. Of course, I know you say that he is a suicide because his orders were to dive his plane into our ship. But, in a sense, I am the same kind of suicide. I have a genuine admiration for this fellow. Too, he is a human being. I find no hatred in my heart for him, and, if you search your own hearts, you may not find hatred for him either. I ask you to help, not because of any future that you and I will have together; but I do want you to know that, in a God-forsaken island in the Pacific, you and your chaplain, faced with the naked challenge to the essential humaneness of mankind, sought a level of rightness that transcends the vicissitudes both of fortune and of circumstances. I shall not give him a Christian burial, because that would profane his own religious faith that differs from our own. But this we will do— let us kneel and pray to our own God in the presence of this dead man, as an act of reverence in our own hearts. This act will unite us beyond all conflict and all madness. When this is done, we will bury him with a headstone that bears no name, because we do not know his name, but with the simple inscription, "Japanese Pilot," and the date. Perhaps this act of reverence is an expression of the right thing in the eyes of Eternity." For a long time, I sat in silence as the words, the terrible words, would not be still—the right thing, the right thing, do the right thing this day—"the right thing in the eyes of Eternity."

20.

IT is a matter of profoundest significance to me that life itself is *alive*. Again and again, we are so completely overwhelmed by the awareness that particular trees, particular animals, particular people are alive that we miss the tremendous import of the fact that all of these particular things are alive because life is alive. It is the aliveness of life that guarantees the vitality of everything that lives. Observers of nature are apt to be much more consciously aware of this than is the average person. A friend of mine wrote me about the way a certain kind of wild apple tree grows in one of the New England states. She said that first one single shoot comes up, and then another, and another, but that, almost as soon as each appears, it is eaten by the deer. After some days, the little area is covered with many sharp, dried points jutting above the surface of the ground—the remains of these little shoots stripped of all their foliage, leaving only the stalks. Then, deep in the center of the patch, one shoot comes up which becomes the apple tree. Because of the sticks, the deer cannot get near the shoot without injuring their tender feet. By the time the tree is large enough for the deer to stand on the edge and eat the leaves, it is strong enough to stand anything that the deer may do to it. Man, too, is rooted in the same basic aliveness, and it is well within the mark to say that the religious idea that calls attention to God's care of the individual has its basis in the very structure of life itself. The injunction against anxiety and fear finds its deepest foundation here. Jesus is no wild-eyed fanatic when he urges us to consider the lilies of the field. "Oh, men, how little you trust God!"

21.

PROFESSOR Whitehead of Harvard, says in his *Religion in the Making*, that religion is what a man does with his solitariness. It is an important and significant observation, for, in a moment of decision, a man is shut up with his own soul and his own resolution. The observation may be correct that, if one has never been solitary, one has never been religious. It is the solitariness of life that makes it move with such ruggedness. All life is one, and yet life moves in such intimate circles of awful individuality. The power of life perhaps is its aloneness. Bernard Shaw makes Joan of Arc say that the aloneness of God is His strength. There are thresholds before which all men stop, over which only God may tread—and even He, in disguise. Each soul must learn to stand up in its own right and live. How blissful to lean upon another, to seek a sense of everlasting arms expressed in the vitality of a friend! We walk a part of the way together, but on the upper reaches of life, each path takes its way to the heights—alone. Ultimately, I am alone, so vastly alone that in my aloneness is all the life of the universe. Stripped to the literal substance of myself, there is nothing left but naked soul, the irreducible ground of individual being, which becomes at once the quickening throb of God. At such moments of profound awareness I seem to be all that there is in the world, and all that there is in the world seems to be myself.

22.

THE prophet Jeremiah says, "A curse on him who relies on man, who depends upon mere human aid; for he is like some desert shrub that never thrives, set in a solitary place in the steppes. But happy is he who relies on God, who has God for his confidence, for he is like a tree planted beside a stream sending his roots down to the water. He has no fear of scorching heat, his leaves are always green. He goes on bearing fruit when all around is barren and looks out on life with quiet eyes." Some years ago I read a most interesting account in the *National Geographic Magazine* concerning certain trees found growing in the Sahara Desert. These trees are not a part of any oasis but stand alone in the midst of the heat and wind, without obvious moisture. It seems that, hundreds of years ago, what is now the desert was a dank, luxurious growth. As the desert appeared, the vegetation was destroyed until, at last, there was nothing left of the past glory except an oasis scattered here and there. But not all vegetation disappeared; for there were a few trees that had sent their roots so far down into the heart of the earth in quest of moisture and food that they discovered deep flowing rivers full of concentrated chemicals. Here the roots are fed so effectively that the trees far above on the surface of the earth are able to stand anything that can happen to them at the hands of desert heat and blow-ing sand. This is the secret of those whose lives are fed by deep inner resources of life. To him who is sure of God, He becomes for him the answer to life's greatest demands and, indeed, to its most searching and withering vicissitudes.

23.

In his senior sermon, a Japanese classmate made a statement about Jesus that all who heard it will scarcely forget. He was discussing the place and significance of Jesus in his life. The closing words were: "I do not believe he walked on water; I do not believe he turned water into wine; I do not believe any of the miracles recorded in the gospels. For me this is unnecessary. But, when I look at his life and contrast it with my own, I am perfectly willing to call him God. A wide, wide gulf separates me from him." It is this kind of reflection that has caused many to make the distinction between the Christ of experience and the Jesus of history. The former has to do with the creative synthesis of all the dreams and aspirations and longings of the human spirit for perfection of spirit, mind and character—the glowing triumph of spirit over matter, of purity over impurity, of holiness over sin. It is the revelation of the highest reaches of the quest for fulfillment. The latter is earth-bound. It deals with a plodding goodness in the midst of ordinary difficulties. It points up the possibilities of direct human goodness in a society that operates upon the principles of selfishness, greed and lust. It lifts the hope of the moral and the ethical, in the midst of the immoral and the unethical. They need not be two different experiences, they may be a single aspect of one dynamic religious dedication. Millions of thoughtful men and women, for nearly two thousand years, have affirmed a quiet faith in both the Christ of experience and the Jesus of history.

24.

"THOU art my son in whom I am well pleased," or "Thou art my son, this day have I begotten thee." The latter rendering of the words associated with the baptism scene in the Gospel of Mark comes from one of the oldest manuscripts. They reveal an interesting and far-reaching interpretation of the life of Jesus. The crucial question is: Was the sonship of Jesus a gift placed upon the first-born of Mary and Joseph when he first stirred in the womb, or was it something he earned in great fulfillment? The question will not be downed, either by the most vehement affirmations of the devout or the careless irrelevances of the thoughtless. For in the answer turns the challenge and the judgment of Jesus Christ. If the sonship was given merely in the fact of birth in some manner denied all other human beings, then it is easy to discern the judgment which his life continues to hold over all other men. But the challenge—that is different. All other men have an irreducible handicap which puts them forever at a disadvantage; and there is given them an alibi for coarseness, for all manner of falseness and weakness. All men can say: "But I had no special gift of God by which I can overcome the world." It is not to meet the problem, merely to declare that all things are possible in his name. The bitter fact would remain that I have a congenital lack in my very nature that puts me in the outer chamber, unless, by some miracle, his power and strength are grafted onto me. This is one of the claims by which millions live. On the other hand, if Jesus Christ won the approval of God in some special sense that sets him apart in his own right, then it would follow that his life presents both a challenge and a judgment. It is clear that God was the answer to all that Jesus sought and quested for in life. Anyone who is as sure of God as was Jesus, can hear for himself: "Thou art my son, my beloved, this day have I begotten thee."

25.

DOUGLAS Steere defines meditation as a voluntary act of the mind. Of course there are times when the mind slips involuntarily into meditation. The experience is like becoming aware of a tune in the mind without knowing precisely at what moment one began to hum it. Nevertheless, it is true that meditation is a deliberate and voluntary act of the mind. Out of the welter of ideas to which one is exposed, a particular idea is selected, quarantined, and subjected to careful and sustained scrutiny. It may be compared to what must have been true in the early stages of the development of human speech. There were many sounds beating ceaselessly upon the eardrums, but certain sounds were separated, charged with unique and perhaps personal meaning, again and again, until at last these sounds became symbols of meaning that in turn were the common coins of communication among people who lived together in one family, tribe or community. To return to the art of meditation—one phrase is selected, or one idea, complete in itself, embodied in a simple sentence or paragraph. All other ideas are rigidly excluded, and the mind is made to attend to it. The idea may set up a "chain reaction" which opens up a whole vista of thought or enlightenment. Once the idea is held at dead center in the mind, one must probe for its meaning. Once the meaning is clear, then one must proceed with a series of interpretive applications to one's own life situation and to one's world. The possibility of application or testing may open up for examination and exploration various aspects of one's own life that are not congenial to the acceptance of the idea. This may lead to a recognition of one's limitations, one's impotency, or one's stubbornness. It is often possible that such considerations reveal the need for a deeper commitment, a profounder earnestness, or a more sensitive spirit. In fine, a sense of sinfulness may be the direct result of meditation. This sense of sin may inspire a conscious need of strength and a seeking for sources of power to enable one to apply the insight to one's life. The search for personal power in this sense will eventually bring one face to face with Him who is recognized as the Source of all strength, God. We need not be distressed over the label; it may or may not be important. Sometimes, the awareness of the meaning of an idea or thought that is the selected subject of meditation will itself cause a fresh inrush of energy which so floods the life that much rubbish is swept away and a clean inner feeling fills one's being. Coming back to the daily round refreshed and renewed is one of the simple, but critically practical results of authentic meditation. Try it for yourself.

26.

WE must find sources of strength and renewal for our own spirits, lest we perish. There is a wide spread recognition of the need for refreshment of the mind and the heart. It is very much in order to make certain concrete suggestions in this regard. First, we must learn to be quiet, to settle down in one spot for a spell. Sometime during each day, everything should stop and the art of being still must be practiced. For some temperaments, it will not be easy because the entire nervous system and body have been geared over the years to activity, to overt and tense functions. Nevertheless, the art of being still must be practiced until development and habit are sure. If possible, find a comfortable chair or quiet spot where one may engage in nothing. There is no reading of a book or a paper, no thinking of the next course of action, no rejecting of remote or immediate mistakes of the past, no talk. One is engaged in doing nothing at all except being still. At first one may get drowsy and actually go to sleep. The time will come, however, when one may be quiet for a spell without drowsiness, but with a quality of creative lassitude that makes for renewal of mind and body. Such periods may be snatched from the greedy demands of one's day's work; they may be islanded in a sea of other human beings; they may come only at the end of the day, or in the quiet hush of the early morning. We must, each one of us, find his own time and develop his own peculiar art of being quiet. We must lose our fear of rest. There are some of us who keep up our morale (morale has been defined as a belief in one's cause) by being always busy. We have made a fetish of fevered action. We build up our own sense of security by trying to provide a relentless, advantageous contrast between ourselves and others by the fevered, intense activities in which we are engaged. Actually, such people are afraid of quiet. Again, most activities become a substitute for the hard-won core of purpose and direction. The time will come when all activities are depressing and heavy, and the dreaded question, "What's the use?" will have to be faced and dealt with. The first step in the discovery of sources of strength and renewal is to develop the art of being still, physical and mental cessation from churning. This is not all, but it is the point at which we begin.

27.

MEN may come to God through nature; it has been said, men may come to God through other good men; but he who seeks God with all of his heart will someday on his way meet Jesus. The greatest single contribution that Jesus made to those who knew him in Palestine was the creating in them of a faith in himself. The deepest tragedy of his life was the fact that there were those who doubted his integrity and his motives. Doubt of this character is unmanageable because it tempts man to arrogance, boasting or mock humility. That men might know his Father even as he knew Him, that they might enter into the fullness of their destiny as children of God by loving one another, that they might live in God's presence with renewed minds and chastened spirits, this was the great desire of Jesus. The answer of the world to his goodness and his revelation was death. But the ages have discovered what is one of man's oldest spiritual insights: death is an episode in, not the end of, life. Perhaps the greatest discovery that we can make concerning Jesus is that, at long last, death could not touch in him that which gave to his life its great significance.

28.

"WHERESOEVER they may be, they are not without God; and where there is one alone, ever thus I am with him. Raise the stone, and there thou shalt find me; cleave the wood, and I am there," saith Jesus. This is often called the Oxyrhynchus fragment of a lost saying of Jesus. The quotation is not to be found in any of the Gospels of the New Testament. It may be from the same record which Paul was using when he said, "Remember the words of our Master, how he said, 'It is more blessed to give than to receive.'" No one knows from what source the apostle is quoting. It is a lost record. The Oxyrhynchus fragment points up one of the great facts of life; namely, that, wherever we may be, we cannot possibly be without God. The fear of isolation seems to be the master fear of human life. Almost all the things to eat away at our sense of security can be traced to this basic fear. It has been suggested that this is true because God and God alone is the only final ground of security and community for the individual. Therefore, all of the sense of penetrating aloneness which we may feel, all of the deep distress of spirit arising out of the tension coming from feeling stranded and cut off, all of the quiet or churning panic developed from a sudden awareness of a loss of props and defenses, all of this is God's way of reminding us that, wheresoever we are and whatsoever may be our condition, we are not without God. The panic, the fear, is the cry of recognition. Raise the stone, and there thou shalt find Him; cleave the wood, and He is there.

29.

"I cannot say with the Apostle Paul that I have fought a good fight, but I can say that I have fought a hard one." Thus wrote a very famous novelist of the last century. Each of us, in his own way, can make a similar statement relative to the year that is coming quickly to its close. Sometimes we are tempted to measure life's meaning in terms of happiness, as if that were the "be all and end all" of life. We have all had our struggles during the year that is ending. For some it has been the struggle with or for health. Somehow, we have managed to keep going, even though there were days when we were sure that we had reached the end of our strength. It was the *fear* of sickness rather than the fact of sickness that made the battle so terrific. We rejoice at the end of the year that, despite the loss of a few skirmishes, we lost no major contest to illness. Some others struggled, lost, and came to the end of the year bound to their beds. For them, there is the joy of survival and the hope of the days ahead for recovery. For some, the job of work has been very difficult. Major working conditions have changed, or perhaps there is a new management or a change of employment in mid-passage. These or similar circumstances have made for new adjustments under grave handicaps. Thus, the year's end means deep uncertainty as to the immediate future. All of this adds up to a hard fight rather than a good one. During the year that is ending Death has come within the immediate circle of family or familiar friends. It may have come suddenly around the corner, or down a long road in full view over many months. Always it is the same—the stark sense of desertion; the shock of permanent physical separation; loneliness, drear and barren. To some, it has come in double or triple doses, hitting ever at the same weakness, fear of isolation. For such as these, the year has been one of tempest and tumult, out of which new powers may have been released into one's spirit, and new courage found. The fight has not been good, but it has been hard. There are some to whom the year has been one of great discovery and fulfillment in other ways. Some things for which one has waited through the years have borne fruit at last. Some battle that one has waged for years has been won this year; some dream that has hovered near for many months, made of one's life its resting-place this year; some door that has closed long ago but at which one has continued to knock, oh, for so long a time, opened this year. For such, the fight has been both hard and good. Each of us, whatever may be our experiences, comes to the end of the year with the melody of triumph in our hearts and the quest for fulfillment in our spirits, out of which we build our hopes for the year that is being born.

30.

THIS is the season of gathering in, the season of the harvest in nature. Many things that were started in the spring and early summer have grown to fruition and are now ready for reaping. Great and significant as is the harvest in nature, the most pertinent kind of in-gathering for the human spirit is what I call "the harvest of the heart." Long ago, Jesus said that men should not lay up for themselves treasures on earth, where moths corrupt and thieves break in and steal, but that men should lay up for themselves treasures in heaven. This insight suggests that life consists of planting and harvesting, of sowing and reaping. We are always in the midst of the harvest and always in the midst of the planting. The words that we use in communication, the profound stirrings of the mind out of which thoughts and ideas arise, the ebb and flow of desires out of which the simple or complex deed develops, are all caught in the process of reaping and sowing, of planting and harvesting. There are no anonymous deeds, no casual processes. Living is a shared process. Even as I am conscious of things growing in me planted by others, which things are always ripening, so others are conscious of things growing in them planted by me, which are always ripening. Inasmuch as I do not live or die unto myself, it is of the essence of wisdom for me conscientiously to live and die in the profound awareness of other people. The statement, "Know thyself," has been taken mystically from the statement, "Thou hast seen thy brother, thou hast seen thy God."

IV

For The Quiet Time

Blessed are the poor in spirit; for theirs is the Kingdom of Heaven.

Blessed are the poor in spirit. What does it mean to be poor in spirit? Does it mean having a sense of inferiority? Does it mean discounting one's true worth and value? Does it mean pretending to think lowly of oneself in the presence of others, so as not to seem to be conceited, proud, arrogant? What does it mean to be poor in spirit? Perhaps it means to have a present sense of inadequacy in one's own spiritual life. The gulf between what we recognize as the high spiritual possibilities of life and what we are able to achieve at any particular moment is the measure of one's paucity of spirit. To be aware of this is to be blessed.

Theirs is the Kingdom of Heaven. Theirs is the rule of God. The rule of God in one's life is the priceless possession. It does not mean that one is holy, it does not mean that one is perfect, it does not mean that one is sinless. It does mean that one has a sense of holiness, a sense of perfection, a sense of sinlessness. It is this sense that is the open channel through which the spirit of God invades the life. To keep the channel open and clear is to be in possession of the rule of God. When I know that I have not experienced in all my parts the rule of God and yet the rule of God in my life is the center around which my life moves, I am poor in spirit.

Our Father, for the truth which Jesus channeled to us concerning Thy Kingdom, we express our moving thanks. Be in us increasingly that Thy Kingdom, Thy rule, may guide our decisions, inspire our wills, and determine our actions. Amen.

Blessed are the merciful; for they shall obtain mercy.

Blessed are the merciful. What is it to be merciful? Does it
mean to be kind? Perhaps not. Kindness has a quality all
its own. There is ever in kindness the quality of gratuity,
of surplus, of extra. It may well be that no man ever quite
deserves kindness; it rests upon that which is without merit,
the basically undeserving, the great overflow by which one
life crowns another with glory. Of course, it does not mean
justice or even righteousness. There is always the element
of balance, or establishing equilibrium, of squaring off, in
justice and righteousness. There is a certain core of fairness,
of accuracy, hovering over the just treatment, the righteous
act toward another. Blessed are the merciful! In dealing
mercifully with another, I enrich my attitude with a diffu-
sion of sensitiveness that mellows it, softens it. The merciful
act is the muted act. There is no particular interest in fairness, in measured dealing. It is like the difference between
raw or pasteurized milk, and milk that is homogenized. The
richness is nowhere, but everywhere! Am I merciful or
just decent? Are you?

They shall obtain mercy. Curious paradox! Does it mean that
if I am merciful I shall be dealt with in a merciful manner
by others? That I shall receive at the hands of others, in
kind, the thing that I have passed on to them? This may
not follow at all, or it may. But that is beside the point!
The merciful shall obtain mercy because they have it already. They are what they share with others. Often the net
result is that my act of mercy does call forth action of the
same quality from others. I become so involved in the

richness of the quality of my dealing that I am immunized against the absence of mercy in the dealings of others with me. My life places upon others an imperative that broods over their own deeds, revealing their true quality to them, pervading their deeds with the richness of my own. It is a great risk but, in the last analysis, it is unbeatable. Blessed are the merciful; for they have mercy already.

Blessed are the meek; for they shall inherit the earth.
Blessed are the meek. Blessed are the humble, the low-in-heart, the generous-in-attitude-toward-others, the unafraid, the courageous. Meekness is often confused with false modesty, with a certain lack of courage, with self-degrading and ingratiating humility. To be meek is to have a clear understanding of one's strength and one's weakness. It is to have a normal self-estimate, not to overrate nor to underrate one's ability, one's powers, one's functioning. Meekness is sometimes used as a device for getting one's way, for taking advantage of others, for exploiting other people. It arises out of a sure knowledge that the attitude of pride and arrogance will be resisted but that meekness will unarm the opposition and win the victory. Meekness used in this way is a form of radical deception, and is not to be confused with humility. Am I guilty? Do I "take low" in order to gain my end?
Search me, O God! Search me!
They shall inherit the earth. They shall possess the earth. It is true that "humility can never be humiliated." It cannot be finally resisted or overcome; for it is an attitude of direct

honesty in relationships, growing out of a knowledge that the sure responsibility is to God and not to the estimate of, nor the impression of, one's fellows. It is an attitude of openness toward life, ever learning, ever growing in a perfection which is God. There is no room in it for fear, for cringing, for cowardice. It breathes confidence because it is the soul's answer to the Scrutiny of God. To such, life and the earth belong!

Search me—Search me, O God!

Blessed are they that mourn; for they shall be comforted.

Blessed are they that mourn. What does it mean to mourn? Does it mean to weep, to exhibit grief? This is the most obvious meaning. What is grief? Is it merely an emotional reaction to a situation which causes one to be sad and in a sense unhappy? Or is it an expression of sorrow, growing out of a profound sympathy for, or identification with, someone in distress? What are the things that are capable of making you mourn? What things, however terrible they may be, are incapable of affecting you? You are blessed if you mourn over situations that are worthy of the outpouring of your spirit. This is a hard test.

They shall be comforted. They shall be reassured. They shall be consoled. They shall be confirmed. They shall be validated. To be comforted does not necessarily mean that the occasion for mourning will be removed. But it does mean that, in the presence of a situation in which there is a spontaneous outpouring of the self in healing and redemption to others whose need grips and holds, the spirit is somehow cleansed,

washed, reassured. It is a paradox. The comfort is in the
thing that happens to you in the process of the self-giving.
That it will do much for the other person may be assumed.
Blessed are they that mourn; for they shall be comforted.
Our Father, let me not spare myself in the out-
pouring of my spirit in sympathy and in total self-
giving where the need of another makes demand.
Teach me the fearlessness that comes from such
encounters.
The results I trust to Thee. Amen.

*Blessed are the peacemakers; for they shall be called the
children of God.*
Blessed are the peacemakers. Am I a peace maker? Do I make
peace in my home? This is my desire. I have a will to peace
—or do I? I must see that no man gives all nor takes all
but rather that, by yielding and affirming, wholeness of
living in community *becomes* the way of life. Of course I
do not wish war in myself, in my private circle, in the wide
world of men. Yet the seeds of war are in me. Deep is the
conflict within. "When I would do good, evil is present,"
or "I want to do what is right, but wrong is all that I can
manage." One slight injury to my pride, to my feelings,
and I let it ferment until it sends a temperature all through
my spirit—a false sense of honor. Sometimes I like to nurse
my wounds. Whole nations do this.
Blessed are the peacemakers. This means that I must possess
and create a will that is good toward myself, toward my fellows, toward life and living. This good will must constantly

be fed by facts and a careful understanding of them—facts concerning myself, concerning my fellows, concerning life. There must be an energized imagination. In my mind, I must play with all manner of creative possibilities in my relations with others, familiarizing myself with the flavor of people and their potentiality. This I must do until there is revealed in them the very essence of what I know of myself. Then I will understand their understanding, feel their feeling, "sit where they sit." My judgment will be tenderized, my hardness will be softened, my justice will be merciful. I will be a peacemaker.

They shall be called the children of God. The peacemaker is so like what men are seen to be at their best that they remind men of what God must be like. They recall to men's minds the thought of the best and the highest. They warm men with the thought of God. They breathe His promise to the spirit of men. They bring to mind the assurance that all stand in immediate candidacy to achieve in fact what they are in essence—children of God.

Blessed are ye when men shall revile you and persecute you falsely for my sake. Rejoice and be exceeding glad, for great is your reward in heaven.

Blessed are ye when men shall revile you and persecute you falsely for my sake. Can this be possibly true? To be reviled, to be persecuted? To be reviled and persecuted is to be turned down by one's fellows. No one ever thinks that he quite deserves it. It causes a man to feel that he is no good, that he has no worthy place in the regard and respect of his fellows because, in some way, he has betrayed them. The most natural thing is to feel that they have betrayed him. But if it has not been my intent to betray them or even to attack them—then what? Suppose I have only done what I had no other choice but to do. There was nothing personal or vindictive either in my attitude or in my intention. I was only speaking out against injustice! I could not stand silent in the presence of cruelty, exploitation, violence. I had to speak out, to do what I could to arouse the consciences of my fellows. This I had to do! It was not in my mind to stir up trouble, because enough trouble was already stirred up. Why don't they face the evil they are doing? Why do they take it out on me? I have no power, I have no organization, I represent no interest. I am just a man who could not be silent, and now they turn their backs upon me, now they pour their wrath upon me.

Rejoice and be exceeding glad. What does this mean? Should I take delight in my suffering? Is that healthy? Is not that morbid? Is that not thinking of myself more highly than I ought to think? I mistrust the mood. Over and over I go in my mind; the question will not down! Can I trust my own feelings, when I take delight in what men are doing to me? Perhaps I am looking at this in a wrong manner. Rejoice and be exceeding glad—because I am being persecuted? No. Rejoice and be exceeding glad because I did not miss my one opportunity to recognize and count myself on the side of justice, truth, right. What a chance I almost missed! Oh! to know for once that I had sheer courage, that I declared myself on the side of decency! That is why I am glad; that is why I rejoice.

Blessed are ye when men shall revile you and persecute you falsely for my sake. Rejoice and be exceeding glad, for great is your reward in heaven.

Thy Kingdom Come

Thy Kingdom come in my life with myself. Often I forget to remember that always I must live with myself. What of me that is unpleasant, ugly, negative; what of me that is pleasant, beautiful, positive, is still of me. I cannot escape from myself. Often I try by a wide variety of means. These escape devices are many. Sometimes it is attempted through excessive work, sometimes through heightened excitement, sometimes through worry and anxiety—but always it is the same —I come back to myself at last. I must let the rule of God invade my relations with myself. What in me makes for disorder, for tempest, for destruction, I must release to the purging, the cleansing, of the rule of God.

Thy Kingdom come in my life with others. Often I forget to remember that always I must live with others. I am not alone, as if I were the only person on an uninhabited island. There are those with whom I am in daily contact. Am I helpful, or am I unhelpful, in what I do in my relations with my fellows? Do I make life easier or do I make it harder for them? Am I an irritant, always managing to be the center of some kind of disturbance? Do I exploit others in my relationship with them? Do I use them as a means to my private ends, sacrificing them to goals in which they do not share? I must let the rule of God invade my relations with my fellows. I must put at the disposal of the Divine invasion the rugged or brittle fabric of my other-than-self relations.

Holy Father, turn Thy holy light upon my relations with myself and with others, that these things that defeat Thy Kingdom in me may be destroyed or rooted out. Thy light sears, O God, it sears! Amen.

Thy Will be Done

Thy Will be done in me. The will of God is often thought of as something that comes into a man from the outside. It is regarded as something against which the individual has to struggle, as an antagonist. It may well be that the will of God does not come from without, as a grand invasion of the spirit, but rather it is welling up from deep within the mind and spirit, taking the shape of the life as water from a spring takes the shape of the banks between which the water flows.

Thy Will be done in me. The will of God is native to my spirit. It is the fundamental character of me. It is the foundation of my mental, physical and spiritual structure. It is what I find when I am most myself. It is what I find when I get down to the deepest things in me. It is what is revealed when all the superficial things are sloughed off and I am essentially laid bare.

Thy Will be done in me. When I come to myself, I am aware of the will of God as part and parcel of what it is that I seek above all else. To know this, to see this clearly, is to understand what sin is, what the evil of evil is, what rightness is. Close, present Father, flow through me in all the ways native to me and all my parts, that, as a whole person, I may do Thy Will with such completeness that I become Thy Will. Amen.

Deliver Me from Evil

Deliver me from evil—in the thoughts that linger in my mind. Evil thoughts come into my mind, sometimes on invitation, sometimes dressed in garments of innocence. My temptation is to deny that they are there or, worse, to think I have gotten rid of them by pushing them down out of sight in some hidden corner of my mind. Once there, they settle down to reproduce their kind. Deliver me from evil, by strengthening me in honesty, that I may give no quarter to the negative thoughts and their residue in my mind.

Deliver me from evil—in desires that are destructive to the vision of the good that illumines my pathway. It may be that my desires are not evil or good in themselves. Perhaps it is what they become when clothed in the deed, that gives them their character. On the other hand, certain desires are geared to accomplish and call it by its true name. In so doing, I would hold it up before the scrutiny of God, that I may see it through His eyes.

Deliver me from evil—in the things that I refrain from doing. Sometimes I see very clearly what I ought to do, but I reject it deliberately and blatantly. Sometimes I refrain by default, not intending to really; but, by negligence or a variety of other alibis, I do not do what I know I ought to do. Deliver me from evil, by stirring my will to action in accordance with what is right, as Thou dost give me to see the right.

Holy Father, deliver me from evil in all the ways by which I shield myself from the wholeness of Thy Spirit as it works its perfect work in me. Amen.

There is in God Strength Sufficient for My Needs, Whatever They May Be

I. Either God is the creator of life or He is not the creator of life. If He is the creator of life, then there is inherent in life all that is necessary to sustain it in accordance with the demands of any particular life span. This means that there must be laws of growth, re-creation, and maintenance that operate as long as they are not blocked. I start, then, with that simple fact.

II. It is my moral responsibility to seek to understand how life operates in me so that I shall not, consciously or unknowingly, interfere with its free creative movement in me.

I begin with my body. I assume that, when life is operating freely in me, I shall be full of health and physical well-being. When this is not the case, the life-giving force that sustains me has been blocked. It may be blocked by faulty diet. It is a matter of spiritual responsibility for me to use my intelligence and the knowledge that the race has acquired about foods to keep the life force unhampered in my body. I must search to find the things that are most useful in this particular and to understand the things that slow me down, making my days demand increasingly greater effort to do the same amount of work. To eat properly is a part of my religious vocation, for by so doing I draw on the strength which God makes constantly available to me. There is in God strength sufficient for my needs at this point.

I consider my mind with reference to my fears. I am conscious of what fear does to the way my body-mind behaves. It slows down my digestion and speeds up the beating of my heart, where there is no corresponding demand made upon my productive energy output. The result is a curious kind of congestion, affecting my efficiency and filling me generally with fatigue. I shall track down the source of my fears, destroy their hiding place, so that the vital energies of God will not be blocked by them. I may need expert help in doing this, but I recognize that that help is also a part of the strength of God.

I consider the tendency toward anxiety. Anxiety arises because I am unable to resolve some difficulty or to solve some personal problem. I must take a positive attitude toward the thing that is the source of my disturbance. I recognize that I am never alone, that I am never left completely at the mercy of the things which would undermine my peace of spirit. God is with me. He is present in the midst of my anxiety, as insight, as courage, as confidence. This I must never forget; God is with me in the midst of my anxiety. Anxiety blocks the free flowing of the creative life of God so that I become undernourished in my spirit and often in my body.

I consider the tendency toward worry. Worry is bad for my digestion. It creates the kind of toxic condition in my system that aids the development of those protests in my stomach called ulcers. Something happens in my organism that blocks the free flowing creative power of God in my body, making for health, strength and vigor. Worry is against life, it is anti-vitality and anti-God. I must remember that God is more concerned about my well-being than I can possibly be. I shall discipline myself in trust— trust in life, trust in my mind and its understanding, trust in God. This does not mean that I shall ignore the things that worry me but it does mean that I shall seek always to understand them; I shall not give them a place in my thoughts that will make me their slave. I know that my life, the life of the world and life itself, all belong to God.

I consider my feeling of inadequacy. There are times when I "give out" completely. There are times when I raise the question: What is the use of continuing to put forth effort in trying to do well what I have been able to achieve only poorly? Sometimes I am faced with demands from others which, with all my heart, I would like to meet, but I fail them. My failure has nothing to do with my intention, my desires, or even my understanding. It is due to a lack of power, of dynamics. I discover at such times that I am depending too utterly on my own strength. I act as if my knowledge were complete and my own power sufficient. I forget to remember that God is my strength and the source of the power without which no thing is possible. Over and over, I must know this: There is strength in God sufficient for my needs, whatever they may be.

I consider the meaning of failure. One thing that an awareness of the strength of God makes possible in me is the understanding that there is often a clear-cut distinction between failure, on the one hand, and being mistaken in the things I am undertaking to do, on the other. Failure may be due to the operation of forces over which I have no control and, therefore, the responsibility for failure may not be mine. When I am too deeply involved in a sense of failure, I am apt to think that always my failure is due to my being mistaken or wrong in the thing I am undertaking. The strength of God enables me to turn even the spear of frustration into a shaft of light.

I consider my desires. I recognize the place in my life of simple, elemental desires which, through the years, have aided in guaranteeing the continuation of my life. They are not bad in themselves; this I know. They are a part of the creative process of life at work in me, a human being. When my desires get out of hand and lead me into paths that do violence to my health, my integrity, my ethical values, or when they cause me to lead another to do violence to his health, his integrity, his ethical values, then that which is an aid to life becomes a corruption. The free flowing of the spirit of the living God becomes blocked and I am temporarily cut off from His spirit. I must remember to keep my desires under the divine scrutiny, and this I can do if I let myself down into His strength.

I consider my desires—further. It has come upon me, with some measure of shock, that many of the things that I desire to do, I do; that I am no better than I am, because deep within me I do not really desire to be better. It is deeply disturbing to realize that, again and again, my desires are fulfilled. I must get the strength to want to desire to be better. I must *desire to desire* to be better. Here and now, I lay my situation before God and seek His strength that I may desire to desire to be whole. This I do with confidence, because there is in God strength sufficient for my needs whatever they may be.

I consider my sins. There are times when I have gone against the right as I have understood it. This means that my wrongdoing in such instances has been deliberate and objective. There are times when I have obeyed a sudden impulse without thinking about it. At such times I have been completely reckless of consequences, without fear, and without an immediate sense of guilt. There are times when I have gone against the right, without knowing it until there appeared before me the fearful consequences of my actions, and I am stricken with shame, or grief, or humiliation. It is when these awarenesses are upon me that I reach out for the strength of God to course through me, to cleanse my mind, purify my heart, and abide with me as I work out the conditions of my forgiveness.

I consider my sins—further. There are subtle ways by which I have blocked the clean feeling, fouled the upright thought, stifled the good impulse, without doing the deliberate act of transgression. I have surrounded my thoughts with fog so that my vision became blurred; I have indulged in half measures, because the clear, full measure required more patience or more effort than I cared, at the moment, to exercise, thus causing the right thing, even as I saw it, to be lost by default. Pride has entered into the quality of self-giving, thus devaluating my motives in service. Then some spoken word, some fleeting memory of a bygone grace—something, throws a flood of blinding light into the remote corners of my life making me aware of my need. I reach out for the strength of God, which is sufficient for my needs, whatever they may be.

I consider my relations with people. There are some people who irritate me. Sometimes I can put my finger on the reasons, sometimes I cannot. There are times when I show my irritation by the sharp retort, the sudden frown, the sense of tension in my body. When I am irritated, I create around me a negative atmosphere, in which it is very difficult for other people to be at ease. In addition, I have a sense of shame because of my behavior, then perhaps a feeling of guilt, and, with the feeling of guilt, the creative, life-giving spirit of God encounters grave difficulty in effecting a release in me. In my effort to overcome this, I must remember that there is, in God, strength sufficient for my needs, whatever they may be.

I consider my relations with people—further. I want to love people with understanding and sureness of touch. Often I fumble. My zeal runs ahead of my understanding. I do not take the time to inform my good will—I am become too anxious to be effective in my relations. Hence, I hurt easily; and instead of having happy relations, satisfying relations with people, I am confused. In my confusion I am apt to say, "They do not like me." I must quit my anxiety, be still *within,* until my sense of Life makes it simple for me to work out informed relations with my fellows. Hence, there will be blunders I do not make. I will have an eagerness for facts and I will cushion them with understanding. In my effort, I shall rely on the strength of God, which is sufficient for my needs, whatever they may be.

I Let Go of My Accumulations

My ego is like a fortress.
I have built its walls stone by stone
To hold out the invasion of the love of God.

But I have stayed here long enough. There is light
Over the barriers. O my God—
The darkness of my house forgive
And overtake my soul.
I relax the barriers.
I abandon all that I think I am,
All that I hope to be,
All that I believe I possess.
I let go of the past,
I withdraw my grasping hand from the future,
And in the great silence of this moment,
I alertly rest my soul.
As the sea gull lays in the wind current,
So I lay myself into the spirit of God.
My dearest human relationships,
My most precious dreams,
I surrender to His care.
All that I have called my own
I give back. All my favorite things
Which I would withhold in my storehouse
From his fearful tyranny,
I let go.
I give myself
Unto Thee, O my God. Amen.

I Accept the Good in Myself
There have been times when things of beauty
Have stirred me deeply—
Sunlight pouring into a city alleyway,

Moonlight upon the water of a still lake.
That in me which responds to beauty
I recognize. This I love.
For the beauty which unites us
   I am thankful.
There have been times when something in me
   Has stopped my telling of an untruth
   Or the exaggerating of the facts.
That in myself and in my fellows
Which desires truth, I reverence and love.
   I love myself.
I stop to reflect upon the finest acts
   Ever performed by any of the persons I have known.
That in them which caused these acts
I reverence. I remember at once
   When something in me has caused such a creative
      and whole-hearted act
   That I was amazed at my own goodness. This I love.
For the total of all the good acts
Performed throughout history
   I give thanks.

O God, I Need Thee

I Need Thy Sense of Time
   Always I have an underlying anxiety about things.
   Sometimes I am in a hurry to achieve my ends
   And am completely without patience. It is hard for me
   To realize that some growth is slow,
   That all processes are not swift. I cannot always dis-

criminate
Between what takes time to develop and what can be
   rushed,
Because my sense of time is dulled.
I measure things in terms of happenings.
O to understand the meaning of perspective
That I may do all things with a profound sense of leisure
   —of time.

I Need Thy Sense of Order
   The confusion of the details of living
   Is sometimes overwhelming. The little things
   Keep getting in my way providing ready-made
   Excuses for failure to do and be
   What I know I ought to do and be.
   Much time is spent on things that are not very important
   While significant things are put into an insignificant
      place
   In my scheme of order. I must unscramble my affairs
   So that my life will become order. O God, I need
      Thy sense of order.

I Need Thy Sense of the Future
   Teach me to know that life is ever
   On the side of the future.
   Keep alive in me the forward look, the high hope,
   The onward surge. Let me not be frozen
   Either by the past or the present.

Grant me, O patient Father, Thy sense of the future
Without which all life would sicken and die.

Let Go of Everything but God

I must let go.
    For so long I have held to the habit of holding on. Even
      my muscles
    Are tense; deeply fearful are they
    Of relaxing lest they fall away from their place.
    I cling clutchingly to my friends
    Lest I lose them.
    I live under the shadow of being supplanted
                          by another.
    I cling to my money, not so much
    By a wise economy and a thoughtful spending
    But by a sense of possession that makes me depend upon
      it for strength.
    I must let go—
              deep at the core of me
    I must have a sense of freedom—
    A sure awareness of detachment—
                    of relaxation.
I must let go of everything.
    I must let go of pride. But—
    What am I saying? Is there not a sense of pride
    That supports and sustains all achievement,
    Even the essential dignity of my own personality?
    It may be that I must let go

My dependence upon triumphing over my fellows, which seems
To give me a sense of security in their midst.
I cringe from my pain; I do not relish
The struggle of life but I do not want to let go
Because the hurt and the tension of contest feed
The springs of my pride. They make me deeply aware.
But I must let go of everything.
I must let go of everything but God.
But God—May it not be
That God is in all the things to which I cling?
That may be the hidden reason for my clinging.
It is all very puzzling indeed. When I say
I must "let go of everything but God"
What is my meaning?
I must relax my hold on everything that dulls my sense of Him,
That comes between me and the inner awareness of His Presence
Pervading my life and glorifying
All the common ways with wonderful
wonder.
"Teach me, O God, how to free myself of dearest possessions,
So that in my trust I shall find restored to me
All I need to walk in Thy path and to fulfill Thy will.
Let me know Thee for myself that I may not be satisfied
With aught that is less."

I Give Thanks unto God with My Whole Heart

I give thanks unto God with my mind.

    I count one by one much that has come to me to make me glad.

    I remember the simple delights—

        The taste of food,

        The tasteless refreshment of cool water,

        The feeling of fatigue followed by restful sleep,

        The friendly greeting of many who pass me in the daily round and whose smiles deepen my faith in ordinary kindness.

    I remember, yes, I remember,

    And in my mind I give thanks to God.

I give thanks unto God with my feelings.

    There are dangers which are now passed—I escaped; how I do not know.

    Vast is my relief that my hunch was wise to hold my tongue, When to have spoken would have hurt far beyond my powers ever to amend or heal.

    The mood that settled was of despair unrelieved and stark; Then a change came out of nowhere. All I know is The cloud was lifted and once again I was free.

    With sheer feeling I give thanks to God.

I give thanks unto God with my life.

    The will to do more than the situation requires,

    The desire to be better than I am and to work at it,

    The urge to be thorough even in simple things,

    The delight in my friend's good fortune,

The sympathetic outgoing of myself in times of another's
  need,
The thoughtful telephone call, the urgent letter sustaining
  the hand of a public servant who serves the common
  conscience—
All these and more are my thanks to God with my life.

The Peace of God, which Passeth All Understanding,
  shall Guard My Heart and Thoughts
The Peace of God.
  There is a peace that comes when lowering clouds burst and
    the whole landscape is drenched in rain,
      refreshing and cool—
  There is the peace that comes when gnawing hunger finds
    intimate fulfillment in food,
      nourishing and life-giving—
  There is the peace that comes when hours of sleeplessness
    are finally swallowed up in sleep,
      deeply relaxing and calm—
  There is a peace that comes when what has lurked so long in
    the shadow of my mind stands out in the light,
      I face it; call it by its name,
        for better or for worse—
  There is the peace that comes when sorrow is not relieved
    When pain is not quieted
    When tragedy remains tragedy, stark and literal
    When failure continues through all the days
      to be failure—

Is all this the peace of God?

Or is it the intimation of the peace of God?

The Peace of God shall guard my heart and thoughts.

There are feelings, untamed and unmanageable in my heart:

The bitterness of a great hatred, not yet absorbed;

The moving light of love, unrequited or unfulfilled, Casting its shafts down all the corridors of my days;

The unnamed anxiety brought on by nothing in particular,

Some strange forboding of coming disaster that does not yet appear;

The overwhelming hunger for God that underscores all the ambitions, dreams and restlessness of my churning spirit.

Hold them, O peace of God, until Thy perfect work is in them fulfilled.

The Peace of God, which passeth all understanding, shall guard my heart and thoughts.

Into God's keeping do I yield my heart and thoughts, yea, my life—

With its strength and weakness,

Its failure and success,

Its shame and its purity.

O Peace of God, settle over me and within me

So that I cannot tell mine from thine

And thine from mine.

The Lord is the Strength of My Life

The Lord Is.

Is God an idea in my mind,

A rumor planted by old tales born of fear when life was young and death lurked behind every waiting bush?

Is God the desire in my heart,

A longing that goes always unfulfilled?

Is God the restlessness I feel after dreams have come to pass And all my hopes have built themselves in facts?

Is God the indescribable tenderness that creeps in the voice unawares,

That steals into the fingers as they linger momentarily in the hand of a friend?

Is God the endless churning of the turbulent sea

Or the steady shining of the stars against the blackness of the sky?

Is God the quenchless aching of the conscience over sins committed

And the vast cleansing in the soul riding on the wave of forgiveness that sweeps all before it?

The Lord is!

He is more than tongue can tell,

Than mind can think, than heart can feel!

The Lord Is My Strength.

When day is done and in weariness I lay me down to sleep,

When fear becomes a lump in my throat and an illness in my stomach,

When the waters of temptation engulf me and I strangle beneath the waves,

When I have thought myself empty and the solution to my
problem hides,
Lurking in the shadows of my mind,
When the disease of my body tightens its grip and my
doctor picks up the broken lances of his skill and
knowledge and takes his leave,
When the tidings are of brooding clouds of war
And of marching feet and humming planes moving in
the awful rhythm of the dirge of death—
The Lord is the strength of my life.
Of whom
and of what
shall I be afraid?

Quietness and Confidence

"In quietness and confidence shall be your strength."
Long before I was born God was at work
Creating life, nature and the world of men and things.
The worlds were ideas in the mind of God
That have been realizing themselves through the ages.
God is not through with creation—
God is not through with me.
In quietness and confidence shall be my strength.
"Acquaint now thyself with him and be at peace."
In many ways I am getting acquainted with myself.
Always I seek a deeper understanding of my true self—
The very core of me.
What I would be and am not yet, reassures me.
Through my innermost self I find my way to God.

I shall acquaint myself with him and be at peace.
"I will fly in the greatness of God as the marsh hen flies,
Filling all the space twixt the marsh and the skies."
What I seek beyond is what I am finding within.
The beyond is within.
The signature of God is all around me
In the rocks, in the trees, in the minds of men.
"I will fly in the greatness of God as the marsh hen flies."
"I will fear no evil; for Thou art with me."
I can never be overcome by evil
Until the evil that threatens
   Moves from without
                            within.

This does not mean that I shall not be hurt by evil,
Shall not be frustrated by evil,
That I shall say that evil is not evil.
I shall see the travail of my own life with evil
   And be unafraid.
For "Thou art with me;
Thy rod and Thy staff, they shall comfort me."